Rose,
Thank you for your love and
support & for all you did for
our mother for so many years!
Love you much!!

Ps. 147:3

"If there has ever been a companion guide to the Bible for those who are currently or ever have been broken, this is it! There are few Christian books that I would call a 'must read,' but this one certainly makes the top of my list. We all have experienced brokenness at some point of our lives, but for some of us we bury it, ignore it, or dismiss it. J. Daniel Moore challenges us through the pages of this book and God's word to find purpose in our brokenness! Having had a front row seat to some of the brokenness the author and his family have humbly walked through, I believe his experiences uniquely qualify him to guide any reader through brokenness to find victory in Christ. This book will challenge you to take a fresh look at your circumstances and experiences to find the power of God in them."

—**Brandon Berg**, Associate Pastor & Worship Evangelist

"In this life changing book J. Daniel Moore brings to life the power of servant-leadership that has been developed through reacting properly to our pain. He points out that while life's pains are very difficult and sometimes debilitating, God uses them to develop our character and prepare us for a higher and more impacting level of freedom and ministry. . . . He helped my life's pain make sense like never before! You'll walk in freedom and peace at a much higher level after reading this powerful and life changing book!"

—**Joseph Cameneti Sr.**, Lead Pastor, Believers Church, Warren Ohio

"So many hurting people confuse pain with brokenness and thus never experience triumph. J. Daniel Moore makes the distinction between the two so very clear and you can sense that the principles he shares are not the result of 'head work,' but of 'heart work.' He speaks from a place of personal brokenness. I'm so thankful he moved from pain to power. I heartily recommend *The Simple Power of a Broken Life*."

—**Gary L. Frost**, The Mission America Coalition, Associational Missionary, Southern Baptist Convention

"*The Simple Power of a Broken Life* is filled with practical, fundamental teaching from years of experience and brokenness. J. Daniel Moore writes as he preaches with power and conviction. . . . With keen biblical insight, he leads us on from our own brokenness, to see God's never-failing love, and *his* ultimate plan for us to experience *his* power through our broken life!"

—**Mark S. Mackneer**, The Salvation Army, Northern New England
Divisional Leader

"The author has been my friend and brother in Christ for over 25 years. I have observed him as a missionary, a senior pastor, supporter of Christian education, and a leader. I consider him a mentor. He has been through the crucible of life and has remained a man after God's own heart. He is uniquely qualified to bring us this survival manual entitled *The Simple Power of a Broken Life.*

The reader will be gently escorted though the process of brokenness, avoiding the pitfalls, and allowing God to guide you in and through the journey to true success. This book will be helpful in learning how to surrender to his will and his timing. All of us will face trials and tribulations. These pages will help you come to a place of rebirth of power as you submit to his purpose for your life."

—**Wayland J. Russell**, founder, Rainbow Rentals Rent-to-Own,
Investor, Philanthropist

"The reality of life is that, as a human race, we are all broken. In *The Simple Power of a Broken Life* my friend J. Daniel Moore reveals that these are exactly the type of people God uses! As you read the following pages you will realize surrendering your brokenness to the Lord enables his work to bring beauty out of ashes.

I am very proud of Pastor Moore as I have been an eyewitness to several of the painful, broken times in his life. We discover, once again, when completely delivered to God, the difficult messes of our lives become the core of God's redemptive message to help others."

—**David L. Thomas**, Bishop, Victory Christian Center,
Youngstown, Ohio

The Simple Power of a Broken Life

The Simple Power
of a **Broken Life**

*The Transformative Impact of Setbacks,
Disappointment, and Pain*

J. Daniel Moore

FOREWORD BY
Raymond England

WIPF & STOCK · Eugene, Oregon

THE SIMPLE POWER OF A BROKEN LIFE
The Transformative Impact of Setbacks, Disappointment, and Pain

Wipf & Stock
An Imprint of Wipf and Stock Publishers
199 W. 8th Ave., Suite 3
Eugene, OR 97401

www.wipfandstock.com

PAPERBACK ISBN: 978-1-5326-7966-7
HARDCOVER ISBN: 978-1-5326-7967-4
EBOOK ISBN: 978-1-5326-7968-1

Manufactured in the U.S.A.

To Paulette, whose grace to this broken vessel is more than I deserve. Of all of the Father's earthly gifts to me, you are undoubtedly my greatest treasure. And to Lucas, Jessica, Matthew, and Victoria, who forgive me for my shortcomings, yet continue to allow me to grow into the father and friend you are worthy of having. You have patiently whispered into my brokenness, brought healing to my pain, and incredible, indescribable delight to my grace-filled life. Doing life with you and yours is the greatest joy I know. Without the five of you, I would never be who I am today.

Your grace, and His, amazes me.

To you I lovingly and gratefully dedicate this book.

He had less now than he had when he was a shepherd, for now he had no lyre, no sun, not even the company of sheep. The memories of the court had faded. David's greatest ambition now reached no higher than a shepherd's staff. *Everything* was being crushed out of him.

He sang a great deal.

And matched each note with a tear.

How strange, is it not, what suffering begets?

There in those caves, drowned in the sorrow of his song, and in the song of his sorrow, David very simply became the greatest hymn writer, and the greatest comforter of broken hearts this world shall ever know.

—GENE EDWARDS, *A TALE OF THREE KINGS*

Contents

Foreword

GOD SPECIALIZES IN USING broken vessels. When he comes across an unbroken vessel he allows it to be broken and then puts it back together again before he begins to use it.

I have known J. Daniel Moore for over twenty years. We became acquainted during a very difficult time, a time when our country, Sierra Leone, was sadly going through a very brutal and senseless civil war. At that time Rev. Moore and his family were residing as missionaries in Senegal. During those difficult years he crisscrossed my war-ravaged country doing seminars, revivals, and conferences, encouraging us and motivating us for ministry. Through his support several churches were planted and built. I will never forget his sacrificial love for our country marked by his humility and generosity.

One instance that stands out is his visit to Sierra Leone just after the Rebels were flushed out of Freetown in 1999. Sierra Leoneans were still fleeing the country when I received word from him that he would like to come and visit. This was a time when most Westerners had been evacuated and citizens who could flee had fled the country. I almost said no because of concern for his security. His words of comfort to us were, "I just came to be with you. I may not be able to do anything else except be with you, but I wanted you to know that you are not forgotten," and that was one of the greatest demonstrations of love I had ever experienced. His humility, simplicity, and generosity have always challenged me.

I came to better understand this when I had the privilege to visit the United States. I then reflected on the inconveniences that he had been enduring during his ministry with us without ever giving any indication of such a thing. These experiences, along with knowing what the Lord has taken him through in the not-too-distant past, lead me to believe that these pages will speak to and transform many hearts. *The Simple Power of a Broken Life* is a challenge to all believers who want to be used by God, who seems to use only broken people. This book will inspire us to take a closer look at our own motives and motivations in life, understanding that in order to be a candidate for the Master's use, we first need to be broken.

May our journey through this truth lead us to the point where we are willing to be broken and fashioned by the Master Potter for God's purposes, to be broken *and* put together again, fit for his use!

Rev. Raymond England
Sr. Pastor Central A/G
Former General Superintendent of the Assemblies of God
Freetown, Sierra Leone
West Africa

Introduction

YOU MATTER! RIGHT NOW, you may be battered and bruised, down-cast and discouraged, pained, lonely, and hurting. But you matter! Your life counts! Not only do you matter, your brokenness sets you apart as being *more* likely to be used to impact other lives because of the tenderness and hope that flows from your broken vessel.

That's right. *More* likely! God is not looking for perfect, unblemished things to use. He is looking for the imperfect who are available. The wounded who will not succumb to their weariness. The broken who have not given up the fight. In short, he is looking for—*you!*

I am living such a story—and perhaps you are, too! A story that involves frustration and pain. A story of failure, hurt, and disappointment. A story of *brokenness*. But my story is not just *my* story, it is *your* story, too. For brokenness is part of the *human* story.

The details of our stories may be different, filled with different names, dates, places, and events, but the brokenness that emerges out of our seasons of anguish is one that is common to all of us, for we have all been broken. Timothy Keller reminds us: "The gospel is this: We are more sinful and flawed in ourselves than we ever dared believe . . . we are more loved and accepted in Jesus Christ than we ever dared hope."[1]

I have failed when I should have stood in victory. I have walked in victory only to be falsely accused. I have missed the

1. Keller, *Meaning of Marriage*, 48.

mark when I knew better. I have found great grace when less was deserved. I have given my best and yet been found lacking. As the ABC television show *Wide World of Sports* used to say, I have known "the thrill of victory and the agony of defeat." Haven't you? And what of the simultaneous mix of certainty, confusion, blessing, pain, joy, heartache, and a hundred more?

Brokenness has many seeds. It's the spouse that walked out. It's the miscarriage. It's the job loss or the failed business. It's financial loss or the crushing weight of poverty. It's physical limitation or emotional weakness. It's the sting of betrayal and the spear of rejection. It's the addiction you cannot shake or the bondage you cannot break. It's racial inequality, injustice, or outright contempt. Those prejudices that seem to be nearly overcome personally and nationally and then rear their ugly, familiar heads once again. Two steps backward. Brokenness has many seeds.

But I have good news for you! In spite of these painful seeds and dozens more just like them, the God of the broken announces in Ezekiel 34:16, "I will seek that which was lost, and bring again that which was driven away, and will bind up that which was broken, and will strengthen that which was sick." Dear friend, brokenness carries with it the hope of recovery from our wounded, shattered lives! Jesus Christ has come to redeem your brokenness! That lost things would be found, stolen things recovered, and broken things healed! True brokenness is to be ripped free of our own prideful self-dependence and the limitations of the situations that beat upon us from all directions.

So why this book? What purpose might it serve?

Because you, too, have a story to tell, a testimony to share. The enemy of your soul wants to keep you bound with thoughts of insignificance, because what you share with those around you may just be the very thing they need to bring them hope and change their world—*forever.*

My mother taught me a long time ago that God always uses broken things. As one author of a few decades back attests: "God uses broken things. It takes broken soil to produce a crop, broken clouds to give rain, broken grain to give bread, broken bread to give strength. It is the broken alabaster box that gives forth perfume. It is Peter, weeping bitterly, who returns to greater power than ever."[2]

I hope you are broken, too. In the very best sense! I hope you will allow the Lord to mold you and break you and refine you, because if you don't remain pliable and soft and tender in his hands, then when he endeavors to mold you and form you, it hurts a lot more. And much more force is needed and exerted on something that is not pliable. But if you are like softened clay, then it is very easy for him to work. If you are hardened, then the strength that is exerted is so much more consequential in its scope.

Jesus instructed: "Blessed are the poor in spirit: for theirs is the kingdom of heaven" (Matt 5:3). *The poor in spirit.* There it is. Brokenness. The starting place in every person's experience with God!

My strong desire is that the purpose of your pain and the healing of your heart will lead you into deeper waters of God's grace than you have ever known before and that multitudes of people will be helped on their journey because of your brokenness.

Here's to believing that there is transformative impact in your setbacks, disappointment, and pain. That the simple power of your broken life will gloriously alter both you and all the lives God wants to touch *through* you!

2. Havner, *Hearts Afire*, 56.

1

Brokenness Defined

> God whispers to us in our pleasures, speaks in our con-
> science, but shouts in our pains: it is His megaphone to
> rouse a deaf world.
>
> —C. S. Lewis, *The Problem of Pain*

THE WORD "BROKENNESS" MEANS different things in different settings. In the context of spiritual matters it is important to differentiate a biblical concept of brokenness from other uses of the word. Spiritual brokenness does *not* mean unable to do something, of no value, broken and can't be fixed, discarded as worthless, etc. True spiritual brokenness refers to such desired qualities as humility, transparency, teachability and the like as we deal with the humanness of our existence. One author put it this way: "Brokenness in daily experience is simply the response of humility to the conviction of God."[1]

The question that must be answered is this: what is the difference between humiliation and brokenness? Between pain and brokenness? Between loss and brokenness?

The world is full of people who have experienced humiliation, pain, or loss—but they are not broken because they have not allowed God to complete the process! And here is the point of this whole teaching:

God only fully uses broken things!

1. Hession, *Calvary Road*, 23.

THE SIMPLE POWER OF A BROKEN LIFE

If you refuse to allow the Lord to break you then you hinder the work of God in your life!

The difference is this: a broken person is allowing the Lord to complete the process within them. For humiliation, there is restoration. For pain, there is healing. For loss, there is favor. If you are broken I have fantastic news for you—God always uses broken things!

But first we must define our terms and clarify what brokenness does *not* mean.

1. Brokenness Does Not Mean Timidity

A contemporary mind might easily gravitate to a picture of a timid, downtrodden person lacking resolve or ambition. But as 2 Timothy 1:7 tells us: "God has not given us the spirit of fear; but of power, and of love, and of a sound mind." The shy, backward, or fearful person is not synonymous with the child of God who embraces brokenness, but walks in authority.

2. Brokenness Does Not Mean False Humility

There is nothing wrong with knowing one's gifts and using them for God's glory. We all have encountered people who mistakenly view humility as the inability to ever receive even the most basic of compliments. Someone offers the compliment "Thank you for that wonderful meal" and false humility replies: "Oh, it's not much. I'm not very good at it" (demeaning of self) or "It's all God" (neglecting of self).

I submit that there is a middle ground between the two where one simply acknowledges the courtesy of another and answers with: "Thank you so much. I am so happy that you liked it!" or "Thanks! I saw that recipe a few weeks ago and have been wanting to try it."

Brokenness is not the false humility that is incapable of recognizing that our gifts have been used to further the kingdom or bless another person. There is no need to demean or neglect the role we play as obedient vessels of his gifts of grace while at the same time giving all the glory to God.

It is neither prideful nor sinful to know what your talents are and to understand your strengths and those things that you do well. Brokenness is not an artificial denial of those giftings. Rather, it is putting them to work in humility for something greater, something eternal.

3. Brokenness Does Not Mean Inability

The broken child of God is not incapable of accomplishing anything. I do not mean broken in the sense of not being useful, fractured, or unfit for service, etc. We often think of something that is broken as being useless or beyond repair. But that is not what is meant by spiritual brokenness. Actually, *in spite of* pain, failures, setbacks and the like the broken saint rises to new levels of intimacy with Christ and usefulness for him.

4. Brokenness Does Not Mean Insecurity

That is, being paralyzed by fear or doubt or anxiety or worry. We are not to be stunted in our day-to-day living or our ability to effectively function within the kingdom of God. The word of God consistently sets forth a picture of God's people being filled with faith, walking in confidence, and empowered by the Holy Spirit. There is no place among his followers for indecisive, indeterminate people who do not find their security in Christ. We are to be people of his strength who do exploits in his name!

Unlike these things, true biblical brokenness centers on the following seven components:

1. Humility

Brokenness has to do with being more conscious of your own spiritual needs than you are with the spiritual needs of others. Mother Teresa once admonished: "If you are humble nothing will touch you, neither praise nor disgrace, because you know what you are."[2] Do you know what you are? Deep down? Do you even want to go there?

Reality check. Let me ask you a question. Whose faults do you see first—those of others or your own? When you observe the short-comings of another do they continue to bother you and nag at you or does your mind immediately go to your own shortcomings? As we draw closer to Jesus we will be full of grace toward others.

Without humility we become puffed up at the wonderful thing God has done in our life and grow insensitive to those who have not walked through the same thing. Without humility we begin to treat others as something less than who they are and something less than who we think we are. Without humility the power of God's unique activity in our life causes us to put our eyes on us instead of the One who gave us such beauty and bounty!

At the very core of the current church I pastor is the following: "The grace-filled life is a life that is not afraid to walk in brokenness and transparency before God and others. The broken lives around us demand something more than a plastic, artificial faith. The pain of our world cries out for something that is real and something that works. That something is the grace of Jesus Christ."

It is fascinating to read David's song of personal confession for sin (adultery and arranging the death of his mistress's husband) in Psalms 51. In verse 6 David confessed: "You desire truth in the inward parts." God is after our humble honesty—not our legalism, not the blame we would deflect to others, and not our excuses! Notice, there is no mention of Bathsheba anywhere in Psalm 51! Rather, verse 3: "I acknowledge my transgressions, and my sin is ever before me." David's prayer (the prayer of the broken!) is not simply "bail me out"! The broken king cried out, "*I* have done this!

2. Mother Teresa, "Mother Teresa's Humility List," lines 2–4.

I am to blame! *I* stand in need of cleansing! Change *me*! Create in *me* a clean heart!"

The humility of genuine brokenness has to do with being more conscious of your own spiritual needs than you are with the spiritual needs of others. You have gazed into the depths of your very own soul and are horrified at the sight.

2. Dependency

One of the great bifurcations of the church in our day is the division between shallow, self-sufficient Christians and those who truly endeavor to live their lives totally dependent on Jesus Christ. In the West we are so fond of the glitzy, the flashy, the easy, that which costs so little. Our penchant for that which is cheap is not exclusive to discount shopping and online sales. Sadly, many settle for it in their spiritual walk as well.

David cried out in the first verse of the Fifty-First Psalm: "Have mercy upon me, O God, according to your loving-kindness: according unto the multitude of your tender mercies blot out my transgressions." Such a sense of personal responsibility for sin and passionate pursuit of him and his righteousness is always in order and appropriate.

The truth is this: *often Jesus is waiting on something within us to break before he can restore us and take us deeper with him.* It must die before he can bring it back to life. What is Jesus waiting on to die within you? Our extremity is God's opportunity!

Rest assured of this fact: Christ is always ready to receive the offering of your life! Others may not see the value of your offering. Others may not know what you are going through at this very moment, but there is one who does see! He is the Judge of all the earth. He will do right and your offering is prized by him. Your offering is special to him. Your offering is precious to him. He receives it gladly with open arms. A broken person is a dependent person.

Like the woman in Matthew 26 who anointed the head and the feet of Jesus we can come to him and say, "This is who I am. I don't have this and I don't have that. This alabaster jar in all of its weakness is all I have that is of any worth. I bring it to your feet, Lord. It may not be as much as someone else might bring, but it is all that I have. Will you take it and use it for your glory?"

God is saying to you right now, "Can you bring me the alabaster jar of your weakness?" "Lord, I have this physical ailment. Lord, I have this emotional trauma from my past. Lord, I have this intellectual deficiency that keeps me from being _____ (fill in the blank). Lord, I don't have the financial resources. Lord, I may not even have a job right now." Can you bring your weakness and anoint the feet of your Savior? And say, "Lord, what I have I give to you." A broken person is a dependent person. A dependent person who is beginning to understand the simple power of their broken life.

3. Transparency

There is a sweet transparency that refreshingly flows from the lives of the broken. A sweet fragrance that emanates from the aroma of their brokenness. Because they are transparent and genuine for all to see they are also able to see the best in others. Sweet spirits are able to see what others cannot see. Brokenness understands brokenness.

A few months ago my wife and I were about to reconnect with old friends whom we had not seen in a while. We were not totally sure what they would think of our current church planting endeavor, which had been birthed during a time of painful transition from our previous church and which some could view as being inappropriate. Although we were careful not to recruit anyone from our previous place of ministry and did our best to walk in love and model integrity we understood that it was quite possible that not everyone would see things the same way. Finally I said to Paulette: "He will understand," to which she replied, "Do you really think so? What makes you say that?" I simply offered: "Because he has experienced his own pain. He is a broken man and *brokenness understands brokenness.*"

As you draw closer to Jesus you will find that your heart becomes more tender and sensitive to the things that touch the heart of Christ as well. Your own authenticity will enable you to be honest and true to who you are *and* to what you see in others. But get ready—such a genuine individual will stand with magnetic pull to other broken and hurting lives around them. *That* is the simple power of a broken life.

Transparency means being willing to risk. It is being honest about our weaknesses, our limitations, and our sin. Too often we live underneath the mask of what we *wish* others would see.

We wear masks of success and masks of our very best—but we don't open up to anyone about our struggles and our failures. We wear masks of self-sufficiency and strength—but we never deal in honesty with our fears and apprehensions. We wear masks of spirituality—all the while harboring the deadly potion of some secret sin. We wear masks of love and "Christian-ese"—while at the same time destroying the reputation of others with our gossip and innuendo. We wear masks of unity—as long as that unity only involves those who look like us and dress like us and think like us and vote like us and act like us. Godly transparency is the remedy for such artificial living.

4. Vulnerability

A broken person carries within them a certain sense that they may be taken advantage of or misunderstood. Sometimes both! But with Christ as the great Anchor of life they courageously forge ahead—not without wisdom, neither without foresight—but forge ahead they must. Even if by doing so they open themselves up to further pain.

No one likes to deal with self. It requires tremendous honesty, commitment, and vulnerability. Such vulnerability can only be accomplished with a strong and firm faith.

As you begin to deal with self, as you begin to deal with the flesh, you will be tempted to walk away because the cost is simply too great. But here is the key—the very pain we dread and at times resist is actually the means by which God brings his greatest blessings to our lives. A commitment to deal with self requires vulnerability.

Yet, as ever, we are not alone. We are encouraged with the words of Paul to the church at Thessalonica: "Faithful is he who calls you, who also will do it" (1 Thess 5:24).

5. Sensitivity

As you draw closer to Jesus you will find that your heart becomes more tender and sensitive to the things that touch the heart of God. Insensitivity toward others will begin to dissipate as will a critical spirit and judgmental attitude. Jesus said in John 13:35, "By this shall all men know that you are my disciples, if you have love one to another."

Sensitivity will manifest itself not only with more intimate times in the presence of Jesus, but also in acts of kindness in our day-to-day living. Why is it that we often refer to our spouse as our best friend but at the same time speak with impatience in our tone and frustration in our expression that we would never dream of using with other friends?

Are you kind to your neighbor? To your coworkers? To the server who brings you your meal? I actually heard from a server at a local restaurant that behind the scenes the other servers fought over who would have to wait on the Christian group that came in weekly because that group was rude, insensitive, and—wait for it—cheap! What a poor testimony!

And what about compassion in our community, genuine is-sues of social justice, and missions at home and abroad? Are we sensitive to the needs around us? Perhaps you have heard the fa-miliar adage that the lost around us won't care how much we know until they know how much we care! A broken life is a compas-sionate life. The simple power of a broken life will transcend such shallow and careless living.

Lydia Smith is a prime example of sensitivity, compassion, patriotism, and inspiration.[3] This kind, courageous woman was

3. See "Lydia Smith—American Patriot and Inspiration," *The Plain Truth* (website), December 4, 2009, http://www.plaintruth.com/the_plain_truth /2009/12/lydia-smith-american-patriot-and-inspiration.html.

born in Adams County, Pennsylvania, to an African American mother and an Irish father. She was a poor woman who had saved a little money by years of hard labor.

After the Battle of Gettysburg in July 1863, Lydia Smith acted upon her compassion for the tens of thousands of wounded soldiers. She hired a horse and wagon and driving through Adams County she collected donations of food and clothing and distributed them among the wounded.

When the donations dried up, she began spending her own money. Each day, with her wagon heaped high, she turned toward the hospitals; and when she reached them, weary from miles of travel, she began to distribute the articles she had brought. To Union soldiers only? No. Union and Confederate alike. In the latter, she was able to see past their role as warriors who were fighting to perpetuate slavery and view them only as wounded, suffering humans. She continued to provide the makeshift hospital populations around Gettysburg with food, clothing and delicacies *until she had spent her entire life savings.*

6. Teachability

More than once in four decades of ministry I have seen individuals with talent, ability, personality, and charm. Yet their potential was constrained and repressed by the lack of a teachable spirit, leaving them far short of what they could have been.

Yes, talent is very important. Yes, a proper skill set matched up with the right situation is of inestimable value. But most Christian leaders I know would tell you that if they had to choose between a person with great talent but who was difficult to teach, or a person with lesser talent and a teachable spirit they would choose the latter every time.

Why? Because the one without a teachable spirit interrupts the free flow of God's blessing on the organization—any organization!—and infects those around them in a negative way.

I must ask: Are you teachable? I realize that we are blessed and we are more than conquers and we are children of the King— but are you teachable?!

Being teachable is really all about our attitude, who we are at the core of our being. Question: Are you teachable? It is the teachable who make significant impact. It is the teachable who leave a lasting legacy. It is the teachable who dare to ponder how their brokenness just might be used of God to further his kingdom.

In order to be teachable we must be willing to listen—even when it hurts! My family and I had the joy of living four and a half years in West Africa. An old proverb there states: "Much silence makes a powerful noise." Do those closest to you consider you a good listener? David Augsburger asserts: "Being heard is so close to being loved that for the average person, they are almost indistinguishable."[4]

As believers, we must keep our ears open to the voice of God. We must hear from the Holy Spirit. And we must believe in the simple power of a broken life.

7. Submission to Authority

Let there be no misunderstanding—an influential life is a life that understands the biblical concept and flow of authority. In fact, *your authority is in direct proportion to your willingness to be under authority!*

But "submission and suffering are utterly contrary to the flesh. The thing man loves more than anything else in this world is himself. . . . Suffering is so unwelcome to the flesh that it demands the total surrender of our wills," penned L. E. Maxwell.[5]

These seven qualities must be funneled through the yielded life of every servant and devoted follower of Jesus Christ. Only then will our individual brokenness begin to touch his power and find its truest meaning.

4. Augsburger, *Caring Enough to Hear*, 12.

5. Maxwell, *Born Crucified*, 109.

A missing ingredient in the lives of many Christians is servant-hood. Altogether, "serve, servant, service" are found 843 times in 771 verses of the Bible (KJV). Our culture is enamored with leadership, but the Bible is all about servanthood. *Servanthood.* Hundreds of thousands flock to leadership seminars annually. But when is the last time you heard of a conference or workshop on servanthood? And if such an enigmatic thing did exist how many do you think would actually show up?

Why does the Lord place such emphasis on servanthood? *Because we always strengthen the value of who we are through acts of humility.*

Ever since she was five and six years old, our youngest child, Victoria, has wanted to be a school teacher. We have video of her in first and second grade lining up her stuffed animals and "teaching" them. It's just always been a part of who she is. She is now in her mid-twenties, teaching second grade in the inner city by choice, excelling in her vocation, respected by her peers, with a deep sense of call and unbridled passion for what she does. A few days ago she sent us this text at the close of her school day: "What college never prepares you for: A student getting called down to the office, coming back, knocking on the door and saying 'Bye, Miss Moore.' I walk toward the door and she says 'Can you hold me?' I hug her and she breaks down bawling into your shoulder, mumbling 'They're taking me. I'm going to a foster home and I'm not coming back Miss Moore!'"

Tori's text continues: "My heart is in pieces. Children's Services showed up to take her to a neighboring city for a full evaluation. Sometimes there are no words, so I just sat in the hallway and cried with her until she told me she was ready to walk to the office."

Sometimes there are no words. There. Are. No. Words. Not for your pain, not for the pain of those beside you. Sometimes the only thing, the *best thing,* that we can do is simply sit with them and cry. Being a servant does not mean that we must have all the answers, but we will need to feel all the pain. We must have a willingness to feel the vast array of woundedness and brokenness in the shattered world around us. Tori's student felt agonizing pain. Tori felt it with her. And we, her family, felt the pain of our daughter, sister, and friend. Personally, I could not be more proud of the way that she responded. Our schools, especially in the urban context with its plethora of challenges, would be well served by a few more dedicated, passionate, Christ-loving teachers that will just sit in the hall and cry with the broken. Our churches need such as well.

The Lord has not called us into his service in order for our lives to remain pristine and disassociated from those in need! The call to ministry is nothing less than a call to get down into the quagmire of life with those who have no way out. Here is his divine call: "Come after me. Be my disciple."

At times we may get dirty. At times things may get a little messy. There may be moments of being in places and situations that we would rather not be involved in. But those who claim to follow a Savior who dined with harlots, sat with scoundrels, walked among untouchables, and mentored the motley will also feel the heartbeat of that same Savior pulsating within each of them. And every beat of his heart within our lives cries out: go and do the same!

One who endeavors to live a life of brokenness before God will repeatedly be given opportunities to discover fresh dependency on the Lord Jesus. Some of these moments are just the result of living in a fallen and very damaged world. Simply living in such a sinful, dysfunctional world will bring pain, rejection, disappointment, and wounds. These, and many more like them, are opportunities for us to rely more on God than we ever have before.

Some opportunities of dependency we receive from the hands of others as they cut and criticize, demand and demean, mutilate and maim. Sometimes, all of that from those who call you "friend"! Offended people offend. Damaged people damage. Wounded people wound people. Hurt people hurt people. They all provide us an occasion to cling more tightly to the Crucified.

And some of these situations of relying on Jesus are the moments of our own making. At times I have cried out in desperation for him because of the messes I have made. Me! No one else to blame. Not working a good and thorough process. Being too businesslike when grace was needed. Reacting in the flesh rather than responding in the Spirit. Operating from fear and insecurity instead of the reality of who I am in Jesus. Living under the weight of unrealistic expectations placed upon me both by others as well as myself. Okay. *Especially* the ones I placed upon myself.

One such occasion transpired in the summer of 2009 when I found myself in a room with seven wonderful brothers who just didn't understand why the pastor they loved and respected, the pastor they were joyously serving alongside of, seemed at times to autocratically leave them out of the loop. To a man they wanted to support and help me (and they did!) but my leadership style often left them puzzled and confused.

You see, the leadership approach I had modeled for me and taught to me and passed on to me, was not totally a biblical model. It was a very autocratic and authoritarian style that at times seemed to be more about "Here's what I need done" or "Here's what I have done" than it was "How may I help you?" I was not intentionally trying to alienate these deacons, but that is *exactly* what I had inadvertently managed to accomplish over the course of eight years.

In stunned and pained silence I listened as one by one they went around the table and very respectfully and appropriately, but also very directly, shared how it felt to try to serve with me when I sometimes left them completely in the dark. I had recently terminated a staff member and then informed them of it *after* the fact. Understand, they were not questioning my *right* to do that as senior pastor. Rather, they questioned why even have a board if I was going to do everything myself?

I'll never forget as we worked our way around to the sixth of the seven deacons, who was a good man, a loyal servant, and possibly the quietest man on the board at that time. He looked at me in total sincerity, sadness, and frustration and simply said: "I want to be your armor-bearer, Pastor. I really do! But I can't be your armor-bearer when I don't even know when you've gone off to battle." Wow. Powerful. True. Accurate. Wise. Life-changing.

Like a divine arrow pulled from the quiver of God's grace and shot straight from the bow of his truth.

I did my best to hear them and said nothing until all had spoken. This was not a "Let's put the pastor in his place" kind of meeting or "We'll show him who's the boss!" Not at all! There was nothing malicious or unscriptural about what they were feeling. This was not a "heart issue" for them. These were friends and colleagues in kingdom work whom I had disappointed, confused, and let down. We were at an impasse, to say the least. No one knew what to do. They had a pastor that they genuinely wanted to help succeed, but he seemed to be short-circuiting the process! And I felt trapped by my fears of what would happen if I let go, gave up control, and genuinely became the kind of pastor they seemed to be desiring. It went against so much of what I had been taught.

Yet, as I listened to them that night, there was a ninth person in the room along with the eight of us. The Holy Spirit had been gently, lovingly whispering to me that tonight was the night to let it all go and simply fall into the arms of my heavenly Father. To trust him. Just *trust* him. Forget about being a better leader or a better pastor or a better husband or a better father. I just wanted to be a better *person* (knowing that if I got *that* straightened out, the other things would take care of themselves). As I listened to them (and simultaneously the Holy Spirit!) I knew that this was the moment for radical, genuine, and transformative life change. I knew that from this moment on my life would never be the same.

Eventually, after about two hours I simply said. "Okay. I hear you. I understand. I need help. Let me change. I'll get some counseling. I'll change the way I do things. I'll keep you informed and work better processes. I'll be different. I promise that from this moment on I will operate in total openness and transparency. I get it." At first, there was a fair amount of skepticism. Could a forty-nine-year-old leader really change in such critical areas? They were stunned by my offer to get counseling and enthusiastically and lovingly supported it. They agreed to give me that opportunity. We confessed together, wept together, and committed to learn and grow *together*. We weren't totally sure *how* we would do it or what it would look like as we moved forward. But we were deeply committed to Jesus and to one another.

God moved powerfully and miraculously as he invaded the room that night and in the following days and months as we journeyed forward together. I felt relieved. Unencumbered. Unburdened. Authentic. They helped me, defended me, and loved me and with the Holy Spirit's help I honored the commitment I made to them to begin a journey of radical transformation. Counseling helped me immensely, a fact that I shared publicly with the congregation. In short, my life and ministry from that point on became about two vitally important things: brokenness and transparency. No more pretending. No more keeping others from seeing my weak spots. No more acting like I didn't need help or that I could do it just as well as someone else could. Just being real. An open book. Broken. Transparent. In need of grace and mercy. All. The. Time. And that is when the seeds of this book were planted many years ago.

Though I have moved on in ministry, there is not one of those men whom I don't continue to consider to be a dear friend. Not one whom I would not greet or hug their neck or sit down and have a meal with. Not one for whom I will not go to my grave being immensely grateful for. Brothers, you know who you are—I love you and am in your debt!

Likewise, this may well be a defining moment for many of you. If you turn back from this moment you may squander years before an opportunity like this ever presents itself to you again. Listen to his voice now! Learn now! Submit to authority *now!*

If you want a better marriage it will *cost* you something. If you want a better relationship with someone else it will *cost* you something. If you want to go deeper with God in brokenness it will *cost* you something. If you really want your life to count it will *cost* you something. Will you pay the price? If not, why not? If not now, when? Let the journey begin!

2

The Pain of Promise Delayed

—ABRAHAM

A dream received seems to ache for expression. Dreams must
be insulated, especially in their seminal stage, from the deadly
frostbite caused by the frozen breath of the dreamless.

Dreams are rare, precious pearls easily trodden under
the cloven hooves of unimaginative and faithless swine.

—MARK RUTLAND, DREAM

DELAY. NOT YET. SOMETIME soon. Some day. The answer is on its
way. These short words and simple phrases can be the source of
some of our greatest tests and trials.

You pray, you fast, you stand true to the principles of God's
word, and then—nothing. Absolutely nothing. You believe, you
trust, you testify by faith, and on the horizon of your life's desire—
nothing. Just the pain—the agonizing pain—of promise delayed.

You tithe, but the breakthrough has not yet appeared. You
initiate forgiveness and reconciliation in some broken relationship, but the feelings are not reciprocated and you shockingly
discover that the other person is no closer to seeing their wrong
than they were all those years ago. You are praying for renewed
passion and deeper intimacy with Jesus only to awaken today
with the same sense of dullness and listlessness that has plagued
you for several months.

In short, it seems that your heart desires more from God and is standing firm until it becomes reality but in the honesty of your heart and reality of your life, well, frankly there just isn't very much to be seen.

Abraham had been promised by God to be the father of "a great nation" (Genesis 12). So in obedience, Abraham waited. And waited. And waited some more. Eventually, the weeks became months and the months became years. And Abraham continued to wait. Even when the years became decades.

A quarter of a century—twenty-five years!—passed before the son of the promise would be born. How often through those two and a half decades did the searing heat of the desert sand sting Abraham's eyes as he gazed out on the lonely, childless horizon of a land he did not know! And how often did the searing heat of a promise delayed singe his soul and spirit while he looked longingly for the fulfillment of that long ago promise! God, where *are* you?

When the promise seems delayed it is imperative that you *not* take things into your own hands and demand your rights. Perhaps no group of people finds this as difficult to do as do we Americans. We who were born in the cauldron of freedom have from our birth been protected by "individual rights." While "individual rights" are proper and necessary in a legal and societal sense, they become absolutely destructive and deadly in a spiritual, moral sense. I cannot embrace him as Savior while clinging to my rights!

The cry of the age appears to be "It's my life and I'll live it as I please," which is in direct contrast to the way of the Nazarene who said, "For whosoever will save his life shall lose it" (Matt 16:25).

Preacher, what in the world are you talking about? I'm speaking of marriages that are being pulled apart because one or both spouses refuse to give up their rights. I'm talking about people who have more money and more things than you ever dreamed of and still it's not enough because you never learned the joy of investing in God's economy. I'm warning of children who are headed for squandered years and unfulfilled lives because of parents who could not give them up to the Lord's work. I'm totally baffled by the fact that over three billion people are unreached, with no adequate witness of who Jesus is, mission fields are crying out for laborers, windows of opportunity are wide open, yet the simplistic prayer of so many Christians is that their children will grow up to be rich!

If your promise is delayed why not lay down your notion of your rights and investigate the things of God at a deeper level? You see, dying to self and losing your "rights" is the crowning glory of the Christian walk. John said (3 John v. 4) "I have no greater joy than to hear that my children walk in truth."

If Christ himself was not immune from painful, wilderness testings, why should we feel that we should be? It is not for you to determine when the desert experience will be over. In fact, most likely, the Lord will *not* allow it to end as long as your only request to him is that it *should* be over. Romans 9:20 (NKJV) tells us, "Will the thing formed say to him who formed *it*, 'Why have you made me like this?'"

I have a question for you. How real is your faith to those around you? Does it work itself out in the painful practices of day-to-day living and day-to-day relationships? Living and relationships that absolutely necessitate regular and meaningful prayer?

Prayer is too important and too powerful to ever become ineffective. Prayer is both asking *and* seeking. You will never get by asking alone what you must seek for. Here's the challenge—sometimes seeking involves waiting. The pain of promise delayed.

Never forget, true discipleship begins, like Mary, at the feet of Jesus. There will be times when the most pressing thing in your life is to sit at his feet and worship—that one, great, necessary thing!

A word of caution here: while we worship and wait, we must be careful not to neglect the wonder of God and our own need to work for the Lord as well. There must be balance.

Some Christians spend most of their time jumping from one revival hotspot to another—but they never get around to actually *serving* the Lord through a local body of believers. There is nothing wrong with visiting other places to be refreshed and glean a fresh perspective, but too many believers spend their time going to a Friday night service at church "A" then off to a Saturday seminar at church "B" then to another place Saturday night at church "C" and then wake up Sunday morning and ask, "Where shall I go to church today?"! Their worship may be sincere—but it is not balanced with commitment *to* and expression *through* a local body.

If you are too busy to work in a local church and to help build God's kingdom because all that your Christian walk consists of is "worshipping" and "being blessed" or having someone "speak a word" over you then you are out of balance and you are missing the joy of intimacy and truly worshipping Christ. Perhaps you are missing the joy that is found in the simple power of a broken life.

Dr. King expressed it this way: "There is nothing more tragic than to see a person bogged down in the length of life devoid of breadth."[1] Without breadth we may enter the deep waters of worship but will be lacking in an understanding of the broader things of God. Without breadth our focus will be intense in the area of worship but nearly nonexistent in other necessary areas of the Christian experience. Without breadth the sweet fragrance of Jesus is bottled up within us and never flows out to touch the needs of those around us. Your delayed promise can serve as a wonderful opportunity for you to go deeper into the heart of Christ. Often, our greatest revelations of Christ come through circumstances that we do not understand!

Friend, how broad is your vision? How much latitude do you allow others to differ from your own experience? Please don't let your pain cause you to turn inward and away from the needs of others—others who just might be helped immensely by your steadfastness in a difficult season of waiting.

One of the greatest disappointments I have observed with those who profess to experience deep intimacy with God is their tendency to treat others as spiritually inferior to themselves unless those other individuals have had the same experience.

For example, good, sincere, godly people travel to some outbreak of revival and have a genuine worship encounter with God and then assume that everyone else is not as spiritual as them until they, too, have the same experience. This may be an indication of

---

1. King, "Three Dimensions."

a lack of breadth in their spiritual walk (among other things). Just worship *him*—not the experience!

Good, sincere worshippers, experience wonderful moments of deep intimacy with the Lord but become so super spiritual that they become more of a hindrance than a furtherance to the kingdom of God. Just worship Jesus!

Jesus is inviting us to journey with him while we wait for the promise delayed. The only way to benefit from its blessings is to stay balanced with humility, grace, and breadth so that from your brokenness you may see him as you never have before.

And because Abraham stayed faithful to the things of God we read of him in Romans 4:20, "He staggered not at the promise of God through unbelief; but was strong in faith, giving glory to God"! Isn't that amazing! In the original Greek the word "staggered" has to do with not wavering or not hesitating or doubting. This verse shows us that when we stay true to our faith without wavering in our trust in God and his purposes—even when they seem to have been delayed—our faith brings glory to God!

Abraham could exhibit such faith because as the next verse in Romans 4 points out, Abraham was "fully persuaded that, what he [God] had promised, he was able also to perform." Friend, don't lose your persuasion that God is going to fulfill and perform his will in your life! You may not be seeing anything happening yet, but that does not mean nothing is happening. Remain unwavering. Remain fully persuaded. Remain true to who he has called you to be even though the long-sought-after prayer appears to be going unanswered.

What is *your* delay? What area of your life is exposed before you right now, and God is saying very clearly to you, "Let me have it. Let me do this in *my* time"? Is it a spouse that you are trying to convert? A child that you are trying to mold without the help of Christ? Finances that you are stealing from God because you are not fully persuaded that tithing works? Like Ananias and Sapphira are you keeping back part of the price? Is it a habit that you refuse to put away? What about anger that rages out of control? These all have one thing stamped upon them—F-L-E-S-H!

Perhaps it's of a more general nature such as an overall lack of commitment to the things of God. Or maybe you are just trying to climb the ladder of success while ignoring a holy lifestyle.

Perhaps it's a perfectly good thing such as starting a new business, going back to school, changing careers, putting in for a promotion, or venturing into ministry. It burns within you, but no doors have opened. No indicators or green lights have appeared. Delay. Only delay. Abraham knew wonderful moments of abundance, but he also walked in agonizing seasons of not now, not yet.

Yes, the pain of promise delayed can be quite intense and the temptation to deal with it on our own terms quite subtle. But we must not veer from the path of faithful waiting, watching, and trusting that God knows best—even while we wait.

And wait.

And wait some more . . .

God must move according to his plan and his time. "Do it now!" screams our flesh, but Jesus reminds us as he did his brothers in John 7:6, "My time is not yet come: but your time is always ready."

And there it is. His time. *His* time. His time "is not yet come." And waiting as a human, limited by time and space, for the One who is limited by neither can seem like . . . *forever.*

The longed-for pregnancy *never* seems to happen. The right spouse seems nowhere to be found. That financial breakthrough is not to be seen anywhere on your horizon. And that ministry, that burden, that all-consuming passion you carry deep within you— well it has been so long since anything fresh happened along those lines that you wonder if you are just carrying around the ashes of yesterday's burned-out dreams. You wonder if you ever really heard God at all.

Yet, there is a divine purpose being played out on the pages of your life. Your collective experience is the book, your trials are the chapters, and your days are the paragraphs and sentences. A higher authority than yourself is the master writer. Hebrews 12:2 describes him as "the author and finisher of our faith."

Before she counseled presidents and served as college president herself (of the school that would one day bear her name); before she served as cofounder of the United Negro College Fund; before she was the only black woman present at the founding of the United Nations in San Francisco in 1945, representing the NAACP; before a lifetime of organizing and empowering African American children and women, was the commitment to God displayed by a life of faith.

Born free as the fifteenth child of her family, just a dozen years after the Great Emancipator's Proclamation ended five generations of slavery for her family, Mary Jane McLeod realized as a young child that the main difference between her world and that of others was the ability to read. After several years of eager learning she received a scholarship to Scotia Seminary in North Carolina, where she immersed herself in literature, Greek, Latin, the Bible, and American democracy.

Sensing that God was calling her to be a missionary to Africa, she completed studies at Moody Bible Institute in Chicago and then applied for missionary appointment with the Presbyterian Mission Board. Standing on the precipice of fulfilling her calling to her people an ocean away, she was absolutely crushed when the answer came back: "We have no openings for a colored missionary in Africa."

Devastated by the bitterest disappointment of her life, Mary chose to make it a turning point for good instead of wallowing in the pain of prejudice and the discouragement of delay. Out of her brokenness, she decided that if she could not go to Africa, she would teach her people right here at home in the South. Her motto had become: "Victory through faith!"

She married Albertus Bethune in 1898 and a year later, Albertus Jr. was added to the family. Eventually, Mary noticed that many black families were following the new railroad down into Florida, hoping for jobs. Her heart was stirred for the railroad and hotel workers living in Shantytowns with no schooling for their children.

So, with only $1.50 to her name, Mary McLeod Bethune, her husband, and young son set out for Daytona. She would start her own school. "Victory through faith!" she once again told herself.

Starting with five young girls and a four-room house that she rented for eleven dollars a month, more and more girls came to learn and Mary soon needed to build. But where would she get the money? Forming the girls into a choir, she traveled with them to churches and hotels as a way to publicize the school and raise financial support. At one hotel, she met a distinguished gentleman with white hair who seemed genuinely interested in her description of and vision for the school. She invited him to visit, not certain if he would accept.

A few days later, a sleek black car drove up in front of the modest little house. That same white-haired gentleman stepped out of the car and looked around. "But . . . where's the school?" he said in bewilderment.

Mary McLeod Bethune smiled broadly and replied, "In my mind and in my heart, Mr. Gamble! What you see is just the seed, which will soon grow. But we need a board of trustees, with men like you who also have a vision for what the school can become. Mr. Gamble, will you become our first trustee?"

"I like your attitude, Mrs. Bethune," he said. "I would be honored to be the first trustee of your school." And that is how Mr. James Norris Gamble, vice president of Proctor & Gamble and son of the founder, became a valuable friend to Mary McLeod Bethune and her school. Out of disappointment and personal pain she chose to stay near her Savior and his cross. She chose to *believe!* And the first building to be built on her property was appropriately named "Faith Hall."[2]

Likewise, as the script of your pain unfolds, allow faith to keep you close to the Author, for soon, very soon, he will reveal his glory to you as well. Remember, all is not as it appears to you. Erwin McManus writes in *The Last Arrow*: "He shapes His will in us far more than He speaks His will to us."[3] God always has more

2. Jackson, *Heroes in Black History*, 83–87.

3. McManus, *Last Arrow*, 178.

options than you or I can think of! There is always more of him
than we can see!

To Adam and Eve in sin he was the Satan-bruiser who provided clothes of skins to cover their shame. To Noah and his family he was the Admiral of the high seas, keeping the ark afloat in
the midst of torrential judgment. To Isaac on the altar he was the
Lamb that God provided. To Israel in Egypt's cruel bondage he
was the designer of plagues, the divider of waters, and the deliv-
erer of his people. To Joshua and his army of greenhorn rookies
he was the puller down of enemy walls. To a teenage shepherd boy
he was the Lord of hosts, the guider of one smooth stone, and the
slayer of giants. To that same shepherd boy who grew to be a king
rocked by the horror and shame of adultery and murder he was
the creator of a clean heart, the renewer of a right spirit, and the
restorer of the joy of his salvation. To Jeremiah he was the revealer
of great and mighty things. To Shadrach, Meshach, and Abednego
he was the fourth man in the fiery furnace. To Daniel he was the
invisible hand that shut tight the lions' mouths. To downtrodden,
discouraged, denying Peter he was the giver of agape love. To Ste-
phen, the first martyr of the church, he was the one standing on
the right hand of God, welcoming home one of heaven's heroes.
To Saul of Tarsus he was a light from heaven on the Damascus
road. To Jude he was "Him that is able to keep you from falling."
And to John the Revelator he was the "Lion of the tribe of Judah
. . . the Alpha and Omega, the beginning and the end." There is
always more of him than we can see!

Despite becoming a quadriplegic at the age of seventeen from
a diving accident in 1967, Joni Eareckson Tada has gone on to touch
the lives of millions around the globe through her incredible testimony of faith and courage in the midst of tragedy. I once had the opportunity to personally witness the deep impact she has on the lives
of especially those who might feel hopelessly marginalized or those
who might feel that their mountain of impossibility is insurmount-
able. Her message? "I looked through the Bible with my mouth stick,
and I suddenly realized that God is supremely good in the midst
of suffering. Not because He gives answers but because He *is* the

answer. He doesn't offer frivolous words absent from meaning; He is the Word and the meaning behind it."[4]

Reach out with the strong arm of faith! Grab onto Hebrews 10:37. Pull it close to your spirit, and do not let it go: "For yet a little while, and he that shall come will come, and will not tarry." He is preparing to reveal his glory and bring you the fulfillment of a promise delayed!

Just like he did for Abraham. "For Sarah conceived, and bore Abraham a son in his old age, at the set time of which God had spoken to him" (Gen 21:2). Did you see it? *"At the set time."* What is that time? On God's end it is the time that he alone knows in the depths of his sovereignty. On your end it is the glorious end of a promise delayed.

Could it be that the heat of your present desert is about to give way to the cool, refreshing oasis of answered prayer? Is it possible that the pain of your barrenness will soon be soothed beyond your wildest expectations? And might it be that the silent ache of your promise delayed is going to be pierced by the joyful sound of the birth of your promise?

Yes, Abraham waited, and waited, and waited some more. But he also trusted his God and stayed true to the promises of that God. And when the delay was over and the promise fulfilled, he called his son "Laughter."

And may your promise delayed soon break forth with joy and laughter as well. In simple and powerful ways in the midst of your broken life.

---

4. Montgomery, *Were It Not for Grace*, 94.

3

The Pain of Personal Rejection

—Joseph

Total forgiveness is painful. It hurts when we kiss revenge
goodbye.

It hurts to think that the person is getting away with what
they did and nobody else will ever find out. But when we
know fully what they did and accept in our hearts that
they will be blessed without any consequences for their
wrong, we cross over into a supernatural realm.

We begin to be a little more like Jesus, to change into the
image of Christ.

—R. T. Kendall, *Total Forgiveness*

"It's not personal," they say. Or "I'm just not in love with you
anymore." Or "Sorry. It's not you, but we've just decided to go in
another direction." But in each of these scenarios and dozens more
just like them, we are told, "It's nothing personal."

Hmmm . . . Really? My performance doesn't measure up so
you are letting me go, but it's not personal? You are not in love
with me anymore. Me. *Me!* How can that not be personal when
it involves *me!?* And that "new direction" you speak so glowingly
about. Can I go in that new direction with you? If it's not "personal" then why can't I join the grand adventure?

Reality, of course, tells us that it *is* personal. Something about us—*us!*—the way we look or the way we act or the job we do or the talents or skills that we don't possess has led to a decision that, in short, what we have to offer is no longer desired or required. And the sting of that conversation and decision can linger for months, years, even decades unless healed by the nail-pierced hand of a loving God. The same God of whom it is written: "He is *despised and rejected* by men . . . we hid, as it were, our faces from Him; He was despised, and we did not esteem Him" (Isa 53:3 NKJV).

ψ

Few people better represent the vacillation of relationships than does Joseph. Joseph, favored son of Jacob. Beloved of his father. Despised by his brothers. Sold into slavery by them after narrowly escaping death at their hands. Honored and trusted by his Egyptian master. Falsely accused of rape by that same master's wife. Imprisoned for a crime he did not commit in a land where he did not belong. Forgotten. Abandoned. Alone.

Like the searing bite of a desert scorpion, Joseph was stung repeatedly by the pain of personal rejection. And always—*always*—lurking in the background was the inescapable fact this life of rejection he had come to know was initiated by his own flesh and blood. How does one deal with *that* kind of pain?

Anne Graham Lotz has written a wonderful book on this kind of pain, entitled *Wounded by God's People*. In those helpful, healing pages she counsels: "Rejection, disapproval, or abuse by God's people can be devastating because if you and I are not careful, we may confuse God's people with God."[1] Let us take care to know the difference. To understand that while his *people* may injure me, he desires only to heal, soothe, and restore.

So "Joseph dreamed a dream" (Gen 37:5). This marked the beginning of God's wondrous, mysterious dealings in his life. He whose name means "may God add" was soon to have blessing and bounty, pain and despair added to his life like few have ever experienced.

1. Lotz, *Wounded by God's People*, 32.

"The first thing we notice about Joseph's preparation is that it began without any advance notice," writes R. T. Kendall. "But when God hides his face . . . He doesn't give advance warning."[2]

Indeed. He shares his dream with his brothers and they immediately conspire against him to kill him. Talk about no advance warning!

He had a dream and we may say that his dream was also his destiny. Though he would one day rule, though he would one day be exalted first he would be rejected. The throne may be your destiny, but God will lead you incrementally in steps.

And one of the most painful steps on your journey will be rejection. Not only does rejection involve a refusal of acceptance, it may also involve being viewed as useless or unsatisfactory.

But even though you have been rejected, God has not rejected you and is not finished with you. Your agonizing days in a painful pit of rejection are not the end. They are painful. They are dreary. But they are not the end.

Walking hand in hand with rejection, many times, is loneliness. Strange, is it not, how friends can seem to be few and far between as you travel a road of rejection? Certainly, our own insecurities can magnify that sense of isolation and we must be very careful to not read into our lonely hours more than is actually there. But loneliness will often be a part of being rejected. It is also very often a part of leadership. In fact, most leaders will tell you the higher you go, the lonelier it becomes.

This is true in at least two ways. First, leadership in many ways becomes lonelier the higher you go because there are fewer who have also walked that same path and consequently, your pool of close friends who understand the challenges you face becomes smaller.

When you worked the plant floor everybody was your friend. There were hundreds, if not thousands, who knew what it was to walk in your shoes. But when you rose to mid-level management, very few of those same people really understood the new challenges, changes, growth, and stresses you were facing. Your pool

2. Kendall, *God Meant It for Good*, 36.

of peers who know what it feels like to be you has been reduced drastically. Loneliness becomes a very real, though unanticipated, part of your leadership equation.

But there is a second reason why it becomes lonelier the further up the leadership ladder you go. One that I did not fully recognize until after many years of serving and leading people and it is this: *it gets lonely because of the sheer number of people who once walked with you and then simply walked away.* Often, firing a hurtful salvo or two as they left just for good measure!

Their reasons for leaving are myriad. Some leave just because they are moving on to the next "new" thing. Some leave on perfectly good terms with a good attitude. Some relocate. Some abandon you because of their own deep-seated dysfunction. Some grow impatient because you have not yet given them / promoted them / made them what they think you should do for them. Some are weighed down, hurting, wounded, and in pain. Some will leave because they just don't like the decisions you have made. Some just fade away.

And the cumulative disappointment of all those "goodbyes" begins to wrap around you like a heavy blanket of loneliness, bringing with it a dozen Dobermans of doubt whispering "What's wrong with me? Where am I missing it? Why can't I ever seem to get this right? Why don't other leaders have this problem? Is my best not good enough? Maybe I'm not really cut out for this after all. Maybe God is through with me."

Friend, Jesus has been there! Followers who walked away. Supporters who withdrew. Admirers who heard the call, counted the cost, then turned their back.

"Then Jesus said to them, 'Most assuredly, I say to you, unless you eat the flesh of the Son of Man and drink His blood, you have no life in you' . . . From that time many of His disciples went back and walked with Him no more. Then Jesus said to the twelve, 'Do you also . . . go away?'" (John 6:53, 66, 67 NKJV).

Isn't that amazing? Even the Son of God watched people *personally reject* not only his message, but his person as well! And seasons of loneliness will very much be a part of the life of those who follow Jesus. We will know rejection. We will face ruptured relationships and fractured friendships. We will know what it is like to see the backs of some we love dearly as they turn and walk away into a future that no longer includes us.

John Bevere contends: "The issue of offense . . . is often the most difficult obstacle an individual must face and overcome. . . . Therefore we must be prepared and armed for offenses, because *our response determines our future*."[3] How *will* you respond? Or should I say, how will *you* respond? Your ability to be used by God tomorrow, your ability to walk in favor in the future depends on it!

So how do we overcome such certain disconnect and severing? Matthew 26:38–39 sets the scene for us: "Then said he unto them, my soul is exceedingly sorrowful, even unto death; tarry here, and watch with me. And he went a little further, and fell on his face, and prayed, saying, O my Father, if it be possible, let this cup pass from me: nevertheless, not as I will, but as you will."

Here we see the singleness of purpose with which Messiah approached his task. In the natural he was alone. No human shoulder to lean upon. No friendly ear to confide in. No faithful, trusted one to whom he could unburden his spirit. His was a cup of solitude.

Yet, we find him faithful to this single purpose, faithful to drink of this cup, faithful to continue in this way of solitude. *If we are truly going to grow as disciples in his image, then we must increase our pain threshold for unjust criticism and rejection.*

And you, friend. What of you? What of the condition of your heart in your hour of solitude? What melody plays its sweet song upon your lips?

Solitude can be a frightening thing if you are not secure in your sonship, anchored firmly to the Father by the strong cords of undying love and determined devotion.

With keen insight, the late David Wilkerson aids us with these words: "The hour of isolation comes when it appears God has hidden His face. . . . Is it possible He lifts His hand for a short while, to teach us trust and dependence? . . . Does that sound strange to

---

3. Bevere, *Bait of Satan*, vii, 7 (emphasis mine).

you? Have you never faced this? Then you have never truly been to the Cross or Gethsemane."[4]

In Matthew's gospel we see the Son unhesitatingly grasping the cup of solitude, for he knew that it would not always be so. He knew that weeping endures for a night—but joy comes in the morning! He knew his solitude was for a season—but that he also was surrounded by a great cloud of witnesses! He knew singleness of purpose in the present would yield the reward of heaven's promises tomorrow! Now he must work the Father's plan! Now he must be about his Father's business! Now he must drink the heavenly cup! Now was his appointed time! Now was the opportunity to redeem fallen man!

Let this marvelous purpose also flow through you, even on the path marked "rejection." May you also joyfully drink of the cup of solitude. May you never refuse such necessary seasons. And may you not shy away from wilderness experiences that reveal like nothing else that he alone is sufficient.

Forge ahead, dear reader! March on, saint of God! Learn to be shut in with your Lord. Keep your hand to the plow. Never allow loneliness to defeat you or destroy you. Continue to bask in the fullness of Gethsemane's cup.

Drink! Drink! Drink! Solitude may be yours today—but there is a crown of righteousness tomorrow! Loneliness may be your lot—but there is a friend who is closer than a brother! Your cup may seem difficult and overwhelming—but it will one day be swallowed up by these triumphant words: "Well done, good and faithful servant!"

Not only does rejection involve solitude, but it also encompasses separation as well. Matthew 27:46 tells us that Jesus cried from the cross: "Eli, Eli, lama sabachthani? that is to say, My God, my God, why have you forsaken me?"

Here we see the Messiah's cup of separation as he is cut off and rejected. At this point, our hearts begin to tremble, our strength begins to swoon, our spirits grow faint. Can we bear this? Do we understand the full meaning?

4. Wilkerson, "Making of a Man of God," 2.

If the cup is extended to us to drink our response can *never* vacillate from that of Christ. We must respond as did he. We, too, must drink! The cup, then, which we partake of, is without question a cup of separation, a cup of cutting off, a cup of rejection.

Supreme Court Justice Clarence Thomas endured a grueling, excruciating confirmation process in 1991. He confirms the reality of a personal cup that Christ-followers will be offered:

> It had long since become clear to me that this battle was at bottom spiritual, not political, and so my attention shifted from politics to the inward reality of my spiritual life. . . . Might I have been *too* proud? . . . Perhaps I would have to renounce my pride to endure this trial. . . .
>
> In addition to suspecting that I had committed the sin of pride, I saw that I was resisting what God had put before me. "Father, let this cup pass away from me," Jesus had prayed in the garden of Gethsemane. "But thy will, not mine be done." The second half of His prayer is the hardest part. Until then I'd been concentrating on wanting the confirmation debate to come to an end, drawing back from total submission to God's will. Now I had no choice but to submit completely. I could do nothing to push the cup away. The time had come to attend to His will, not mine. I could not know whether doing so would make the experience less difficult, but I had faith that His transcendent purpose would sustain me to the end of it—and beyond. He had never failed me. Even in my darkest hours, even when I openly rejected Him, His forgiving and sustaining Grace had always been there.[5]

Friend, your walk with Jesus will be one that knows the pain of these things. Never forget! Jesus, too, was "despised and rejected of men" (Isa 53:3). Your friends and even your own family members will cut you off. Your lifestyle will convict them and they will want nothing to do with you. You will feel isolated, separated, unwanted—*which is exactly the position of one who is nailed to a cross!*

Reflect for a moment with me on the fact of Christ's separated life. Incarnated in human flesh—separated through time and

5. Thomas, *My Grandfather's Son*, 254–55.

space from his Father. Born in a borrowed manger—separated from a crowded world that couldn't care less. Raised by working-class parents—separated from the riches and possessions of a wealthier, nobler class. Betrayed by the kiss of a loved one in Gethsemane—separated from his closest of friends. Rejected by a religious mob from the nation he came to save—separated from his own flesh and blood. Hanging alone as a common criminal on Calvary's cruel tree—separated from the world he came to redeem. Lying in a borrowed tomb—separated from his rightful place of authority. Our Lord's *entire life* was marked by separation, loneliness, and rejection.

One of the most critical things I hope that you will glean from this book is the simple principle found in John 18:2: "And Judas also, who betrayed him, *knew the place*; for Jesus often resorted there with his disciples." Did you catch that? Did you see it? Judas knew the place! Please let this sink deep down into your spirit: *Our betrayers are close enough to us to know our "places"!*

That's why it hurts so much. That's why the pain seems to linger. A passing stranger who throws out false accusations or scorn can easily be dismissed and brushed aside with a smile on our face and no dagger in our heart.

But betrayal from those who are close, those who know us— *us!*—those whom we love and who know our places—*that* is a pain and a stab in our heart that hurts like no other. Beth Moore touches on this: "His betrayer, Judas, had to come from His own close circle. *Betrayal betrays a certain camaraderie.* . . . As New Testament believers, we will find that enduring this brand of pain is a profoundly impactful way we fellowship in the suffering of Christ."[6]

What then, are we to do with such anguish and discomfort? That answer is both difficult and at the same time simple. Difficult to do, simple to receive. The answer, as always in such things, is love. Love! Compassion is the hallmark quality of one who is committed to Jesus Christ. Therefore, by contrast, if one is not full of compassion toward others what does that really say about the level

---

6. Moore, foreword to Lotz, *Wounded by God's People*, 12 (emphasis mine).

of their commitment to God? 1 Peter 3:8: "Finally, all of you be of one mind, having compassion for one another; love as brothers, be tenderhearted, be courteous" (NKJV).

The Bible in general, and the teachings of Jesus in particular, make it absolutely clear that we are to love people. Not just the ones who are like us—but the ones who do us wrong. Not just the ones who are easy to love—but the difficult ones as well. Not just the lovely—but the unlovely, unloved, and unclean. Not just when it is convenient—but when it costs us something. If we know anything about Calvary we know that it was the place of a great and costly love—a place of abandon, a place of compassion.

May I share with you a key to success in life? Always try to see the good in another person. No, that doesn't mean we become naive or turn a blind eye to shortcomings. Remember, we never deal with reality by pretending it does not exist. But it does mean that whenever possible, our first impulse should be to see the good.

When you are praying for someone else or trying to find a way to bless them, start by recalling the good and it will warm your heart and give you a connection with them that places you in a position to better understand them and when we become better at understanding others we become better at understanding their needs and better at praying for them. Philippians 2:3 extols: "In lowliness of mind let each esteem others better than themselves." I don't know about you, but I have always found in my life that when I begin to think of good things and good qualities and good times together with another person it softens my heart toward them and brings a sense of emotional warmth and a sense of the grace of Jesus.

Romans 12:10 teaches that we should "be kindly affectioned one to another with brotherly love; in honor preferring one another." Recall the good—even in those who may have hurt you the most. Forgiving others and releasing the bad, the hurt, the wound, the offense is not always easy to do.

We are not specifically aware of any of the Apostle Paul's shortcomings, but we know from his writings and other passages of the New Testament that he had a very strong personality, was most likely headstrong, and might at times have been viewed as abrasive.

We know from Acts 15 that he and Barnabas had a strong disagreement, a significant difference of opinion, and parted ways.

You see, conflict has always been a part of the human story—even among God's people! Therefore, don't be surprised when it happens and under no circumstances should you pretend that it doesn't happen. Yes, seek peace and unity at all times, but understand that sometimes good people simply see things very differently. That means if somewhere along the line someone has wounded you and offended you, you have but one choice as a follower of Jesus Christ—forgive it and release it! Let me just tell you straight up: If you are an easily offended person, you are not yet broken! Broken people relate to the pain of others. Unbroken people are all about themselves. True brokenness will change your routine of living!

Reality check. Ask yourself one simple question: "How offend-able am I?" If in the honesty of your soul you don't like the answer perhaps it's time to ask yourself, "Am I truly broken?" Friend, God wants to take you past your pain, past your brokenness, to the very core of who you are in order to use you for his eternal purpose.

Please hear this: *offense is the incubator of deception!* What does an incubator do? It keeps things warm and protected so that the eggs may hatch or the newborn may survive. And every time you repeat your wound and retell the story of your offense you are keeping it warm and alive until one day it will hatch into full-blown deception! Forgive it and release it!

But notice this: recalling the good will help you to release the bad! That's how it works!

Several years ago a majority of deacons at the church I had been serving for several years decided that our congregation would be better served by a change in leadership. These were brothers in Christ who loved the Lord dearly and served him faithfully. Their request for my resignation came suddenly and totally without warning. I had made mistakes during my tenure there and they felt that I was no longer effective. As you might imagine, the pain I felt was deep and immense. My world had collapsed! I thought that I would serve another twenty years or so at that assignment and finish my ministry there, should the Lord allow.

Now, seemingly out of nowhere, these dear Christian brothers and I saw things very, very differently. Though their process was, I believe, flawed, secretive, and not born of the Spirit, these were the final words I shared with them in our final meeting together: "Brothers, someday, when a few pages of the calendar have turned and there are a few more white hairs on our heads, we will forget the pain of this moment and remember only the good times of prayer together, serving together, laughing together and enjoying one another's company together." I am grateful for the Spirit's supernatural enabling and grace that helped me to say that. My heart was broken, my spirit was crushed, and I was deeply hurt. But as one who claims to follow a man who was beaten, spit upon, and unjustly nailed to a cross I really had no other choice. Recall the good and release the bad. Forgive it, release it, and move on.

I wonder—who is waiting for you to do that for them?

ψ

Likewise, we must be about our Father's business of helping to remove the sediment of other people's lives and the things that have accumulated there over the course of years. All the baggage and pain and hurts and wounds and bondages and sinful impulses—all of these and a hundred more beside must be met with the love of Jesus through our love! The junk and the bandages and the dirty dressings must come off! We must help to remove them! The simple power of a broken life.

It has been suggested that a person's worth is measured not in the amount of servants they have, but in the number of people they *serve*! Personal rejection hurts. There is no escaping that brutal fact. Yet, out of that pain may be given an increased capacity to pour out love to others—at times even to the Judas that betrayed you with a phony kiss!

In Matthew 5:44-45 Jesus taught: "But I say unto you, love your enemies, bless them that curse you, do good to them that hate you, and pray for them who despitefully use you, and persecute you; that you may be the children of your Father, who is in heaven."

Such love will not always come easily. Yet he is near and he will assist and bless every endeavor to love as he loved. What you cannot do he is able to do *through* you, for he is not only your Savior but your enabler as well. What he asks you to do he will give you the grace to do. You *can* do it!

How many people can say that they have been served by you? How many can say that you have helped to remove their flaws and their wounds? How many would say that if not for you they would still be bound by the weight and the burden of some heavy load? *Dreamers create dreamers! Dreamers do not glory in the failure of others.*

Grasping Christ, giving Jesus higher priority in our lives, means that we let go of our hurts, our wounds, our offenses, our desire to be pain free. We let go of our preferences, our comfort, and what we feel is best and embrace what our King asks us to do. As Chesterton once remarked: "The Christian ideal has not been tried and found wanting. It has been found difficult and left untried."[7]

If you have been touched with this divine kind of love then it is absolutely imperative that you give it out as well. It is the wounded child of God that is best able to minister to the needs of others. So, don't waste your wounds—use them for Jesus!

Don't wait for some person to deserve your grace—just give it to them. Right now! Will you this week—maybe even right now—begin the process of reconciliation with one who needs to feel your compassion? Too often we wait for the other person to make the first move. A broken life is always willing to make the first move. The kingdom of God is bigger than just this moment!

Joseph spent long seasons in prison. Unjustly. Unfairly. But like him, even though in confinement, God will find a way to cultivate his gifts in you! Those days in prison were days of preparation for greater use of what God had given him! Those two-plus years in prison were God's season of working in his life! You see, prison experiences do something for the Joseph's and Paul's of this world.

7. Chesterton, *What's Wrong with the World*, 18.

I heard my wife, Paulette, warn in a sermon once: "Don't confuse the promises of God with a place because he is faithful to his promises wherever we are! In some ways his presence is felt even greater in the hard place."

I do not know what prison you may be facing—a prison of false accusation, a prison of loneliness, a prison of physical pain or financial torment, a prison of despair, a prison of grief. But whatever kind of prison it is, never lose sight of the fact that there is promotion on the other side of your prison!

A word of caution. When you finally get back to the palace, please remember this: Your promotion is not a time for revenge, neither to revel in your past misery. Humility, as ever, is the order of the day.

ψ

The years had passed and the sovereignty of God directed the steps of Joseph's brothers back into his very presence. Famine throughout that part of the world drove the rejecting brothers into the company of the rejected. Unknown to them, a heavenly destiny had sent Joseph to the very palace of Egypt where he served as second in command to Pharaoh himself.

No longer a seventeen-year-old rejected dreamer, he now stands as the thirty-year-old chief executive officer of Egypt.

And . . .

They have no idea at all who he is. Three separate times they bow before the one whom they said they would never bow to (Gen 42:6; 43:26; 44:14). In this way, Joseph, about whom nothing negative is recorded for us in Scripture, is a wonderful preview of Christ himself. Beloved son of his father, rejected servant, then exalted Savior.

Finally, Joseph could bear it no longer. The pain of a lifetime of rejection gave way to his intense longing for reconciliation. The lacerations of his wounded heart yielded to the possibility of restored relationship.

A geyser of emotion exploded from the depths of his soul. Grief intertwined with grace. Sorrow mingled with hope. Betrayal mixed with potential. Yes, it was risky. Yes, Joseph was quite vulnerable. No, there was no guarantee the forgiveness he offered would be reciprocated. But Joseph could do, would do, nothing else. God had been so overwhelmingly gracious to him. He now would take a giant step of faith. He would do the unthinkable. He would conquer once and for all his mountain of personal rejection. Whether or not his brothers would surmount that mountain with him was beyond his control, but *he* would reach that summit. He would move on. He would heal. He would choose—*choose!*—to forgive.

His words are recorded for us: "Am I in the place of God? But as for you, you meant evil against me; but God meant it for good, in order to bring it about as it is this day, to save many people alive" (Gen 50:19–20 NKJV).

Joseph teaches us that even in a strange place brought about by painful circumstances you still have your choice, you still have your faith, and you still have the grace and favor of God upon your life!

Some people are so stuck in yesterday's pain that they cannot see tomorrow's gain! They are so bound up in their misery that they cannot see their recovery! But *you are either living in your history or moving toward your destiny!* Which will it be?

Like Joseph, we too, will go through valleys of rejection and lonely pits of despair on the way to our dream. But when we extend grace it changes us. Placating does not change us. Pretending does not change us. Pouting most certainly does not change us. Only grace at work in the secret places can accomplish such a difficult and divine task. Compassion means that we are willing to become vulnerable. Even to a group of brothers who nearly killed you.

The simple, beautiful, life-giving power of a broken life.

4

The Pain of Unspeakable Loss

—Job

> We have then forgotten that the cross means rejection and shame as well as suffering. The cross means sharing the suffering of Christ to the last and to the fullest. The first Christ-suffering which every man must experience is the call to abandon the attachments of this world.
>
> When Christ calls a man, he bids him come and die.
>
> —Dietrich Bonhoeffer, *The Cost of Discipleship*

THE NEWS COULD NOT have been worse nor its timing more pungent. First one, then another, ultimately four in all, messengers arrived in hurried succession, each one seeming to expand upon the depth of his predecessors' heart-wrenching news. Job's pulse quickened, the knot in his stomach tightened, and his eyes moistened as he felt the cumulative weight of his own personal Armageddon—it was gone. All of it. All the flocks. All the servants. All ten of his children. Gone. All his security. All that he owned. All of his wealth. His future. His dreams. His life. Gone. Everything. *Everything!* Gone.

In stunned silence and on the verge of a total psychotic break he collapses into a heap that only faintly resembled the man he was just moments ago. Head spinning, diaphragm heaving, lungs bursting he mentally grapples to make sense of the hell that has

THE PAIN OF UNSPEAKABLE LOSS

just been unleashed on his ears and soul. And as he pours out the anguish of his nightmare he places himself at the head of the line of those broken, battered souls who have crawled their way out of the terror and the trauma of unspeakable loss.

Thomas à Kempis speaks of "the royal way of the cross" and exhorts with these words: "Do you think you can escape that which no mortal could ever avoid? Which of the saints in the world was without cross and tribulation? . . . And why do you seek any other way than this royal way, which is the way of the cross?"[1]

As those who identify themselves as followers of Jesus Christ we will be granted opportunities to drink of the Father's cup and to partake of the sufferings of his Son. This, of course, goes against our natural side, for by nature we seek comfort, ease, and freedom from pain. In the spiritual realm, however, different lines are drawn. Unseen forces move among us. A higher drama is being played out. A nobler purpose being fulfilled, and the call comes forth as it did to Timothy of old, "Endure hardness, as a good soldier of Jesus Christ" (2 Tim 2:3).

Now, no one in their right mind purposely looks for more suffering. The point is that the mature saint is aware that suffering is part of the plan and therefore does not faint in the day of adversity. Jesus himself exhorted in Luke 9:22, "The Son of man must *suffer* many things, and be rejected by the elders and chief priests and scribes, and be slain." He was able to see the bigger picture.

And while Job's understanding was quite murky at times, there was still something within him that tenaciously held onto hope in spite of all that he had lost. The simple power of his broken life reaches across the centuries to your situation and your heartache to plant some seed—however tiny or embryonic it might be—into the fertile soil of your unspeakable loss.

At times this particular pain will seem nearly unbearable. Its weight suffocating and crushing. Stripped of all self-sufficiency and confidence in self we find ourselves pouring out our anguish to the only One who can truly empathize and understand. We turn to Christ and off-load our soul's complaint.

1. Thomas à Kempis, *Of the Imitation of Christ*, 88.

Allow your loss to produce an authenticity within that deepens your connection to Jesus. Never forget that the Scriptures enjoin: "You desire truth in the inward parts" (Ps 51:6), or "I know that you delight to set your truth deep in my spirit. So come into the hidden places of my heart and teach me wisdom" (TPT). God is after our honesty—not a freshened-up version of yesterday's mask!

Hear also the grand cry from the very soul of Paul: "That I may know him, and the power of his resurrection, and the fellowship of his sufferings" (Phil 3:10). The word fellowship comes from the Greek word *koinonia* and means "communion, fellowship, partnership, sharing in common."

The knowledge of the Risen One then, is the exalted understanding that we are to share in common with his sufferings! His cup becomes my cup. His suffering becomes my honor. His pain becomes my pattern. His agony becomes my glory. His loss becomes my joy. Can you say with Paul, "I'll take the remainder of Christ's sufferings! I'll gladly give my body, soul, and spirit for his eternal purposes! No cost too great, no cross too heavy, in order that I may know him!" In doing so, we find that the pain of unspeakable loss begins to find its deepest healing from the nail-pierced hands of the Nazarene.

Make no mistake about it—the invitation to partake of the bread of Communion which symbolizes the body of Jesus is an invitation to brokenness. Not glamour, not fame, not wealth, and above all—certainly not your rights. It is an invitation to fully and completely yield your will and place it under the authority of the One whose body was crushed. The *fellowship* of his sufferings.

Notice, the first chapter of Job's story states that God saw Job as blameless, one who feared God, and turned away from evil. God *knew* Job's heart! Why is it, then, that when suffering comes our way many times our first inclination is to wonder if God is displeased with us?!

Not only does the Lord know our hearts, he also just may be so pleased with us that the test is *his idea!* You need not worry about going under. Don't worry about if you will make it through the test or not. Even Satan himself knows that God has a hedge of protection around you and *Satan can never go beyond what God allows! He can never touch you unless God permits!*

Have a grateful heart of submission before the Lord and also take a strong posture of spiritual aggression against the enemy! Most Christians do one or the other. But if you only do one or the other you are only fighting with half of the equation, you are only fighting with half of a sword! Discern the difference and know which is which.

There is no inconsistency with God for allowing such suffering. Only a genuine test such as Job experienced could reveal whether he served God from integrity of heart or because God protected him from such things.

You see, the deepest most intimate lessons we learn in life come as we walk with humility through our pain. Pain and humility are the best of friends. And if we will receive them together, great lessons and great usefulness will follow in their wake.

Some people endure their pain but are not clothed with humility. They are bitter or caustic or resentful or angry or vengeful. Oh, they make it through their season of pain, but they leave a lot of wounded people behind them.

Others walk in humility but are not very good at dealing with pain. They won't offend anybody with their rough edges or sharp tongue, they will just wear them out by rehearsing their story over and over and over and over again.

I want to plead with you to receive both pain and humility together. Pain should lead you to new depths of humility and humility should help to soften the sting of your pain! But you must receive them!

Your pain, your weakness, your inability is *not* proof that you are defeated. Quite the contrary! Your pain may be about to give way to your finest hour!

Winston Churchill's biography, *Warlord*, recounts the words of British MP Sir Geoffrey Shakespeare following the retreat from Dunkirk in 1940: "It will be the great Paradox of history that Britain was never so strong as she was at the moment of her greatest weakness."[2]

Pain and humility will eventually come to visit each of us. God has purposes for your benefit that can only come through the difficult and arduous path of testing. But like Britain, your greatest weakness will yield your greatest strength!

And while you walk down the path of unspeakable loss please know that there will be much that you do not understand. It is okay to not understand everything, to not know everything, to wonder what God is trying to accomplish, and to wonder how it will all work out. But you must continue to worship even while you wonder!

Keep your attitude right. Don't become bitter, negative, sour, and ugly. John Maxwell reminds us that "your attitude toward failure determines your altitude after failure"![3]

I know you can worship on the mountaintop—but how is your song in the valley? I understand that you praise him joyously when all is well—but how high are your hands when life doesn't make sense? I realize that you are in church when life is good, work is good, and God is good—but how good is your consistency when you have lost it all?

Keep your attitude right—even while you wonder. Even when it doesn't make sense. Even when it seems all is lost. Worship while you wonder! Stand tall when you've lost it all! Job's worship was the *last thing* Satan wanted to hear!

ψ

Job cried (23:3), "Oh, that I knew where I might find him, that I might come even to his seat!" Is this not the cry within many of us at this very moment? A cry that is not born of doubt or unbelief, but a cry that arises from the pain and anguish of your soul in the midst of your present situation and something within you bubbles to the surface and cries out, "Oh, God! I need you! I need to feel

2. D'Este, *Warlord*, 432.
3. Maxwell, *Failing Forward*, 140.

your presence! I need your healing touch! I need a miracle, Lord! Oh, that I knew where I might find him!" Those of you who are walking through just such a valley must not neglect the presence of the Lord, *you must draw closer!*

As you well know, any journey into the unknown carries aspects of risk and vulnerability. Yes, change can be frightening. But ask yourself this question: "Can I dare to believe that God intends something better for me than my current state of affairs?" What if your current unspeakable, unfathomable pain is also a springboard to a season of incredible blessing and usefulness? What if today's loss is not the end, but the first chapter of a brand-new story?

Too many believers today are living in the land of yesterday's wonder. Let me ask you a question. When you think of a time when God was doing mighty things by his Spirit does your mind go back to the 1980s? The 1990s? If so, you need a fresh experience!

There's nothing wrong with recalling the past blessings of God, but if your most recent experience of God's wonder was what he did for you way back when, then your "wonder" is thirty or forty years old! Perhaps your loss has been allowed into your life to draw you back to your first love and the fresh experience that awaits you.

Painful valleys of great loss help us to grasp Christ and release other things, lesser things. Unfortunately, our great temptation is to grasp things and release Christ! *We must live a life of releasing grasp!* Like Job, you may be asked to lay down some things in your valley of unspeakable loss that mean more to you than anything else. You may be asked to lay them aside and trust in the sufficiency of his grace. It may be family and loved ones. It may be talents and abilities. Maybe finances, possessions, or things. Perhaps your job, your vocation, or even your calling. It may be some form of ministry or service.

And when Christ asks you to lay it aside, the pain may almost be unbearable. But lay it down you must, if he has spoken! To hold onto what he has given you when he asks you to lay it down is nothing less than disobedience. Before Jesus can reveal his glory in your life, he must first find an obedient vessel that has held back nothing from the Master's call. Never forget—who was it that gave those gifts to you in the first place? And once you have laid it all at his pierced feet you too will sing with the sweet-singer of Israel: "You have delivered my soul from death" (Ps 56:13).

The pain of loss and the periods of grief at times settle in on our soul and spirit like a cloud of heavy darkness. But please understand, darkness is not a sign of God's absence, neither that he is unconcerned. Often it is simply a test of our love and devotion even though the path we walk is not always clear. Remember, the greater the darkness, the more glorious the coming of the light!

The Genesis record bears this out. "In the beginning God created the heaven and the earth. And the earth was without form, and void; and darkness was upon the face of the deep. And the Spirit of God moved upon the face of the waters. And God said, Let there be light: and there was light" (1:1–3). The first thing the Spirit brings is light!

I'm sure that Job wondered many times, "Where is God in all of this?" The Sabeans stole his oxen and asses and killed his servants: "God where are you?" Fire fell from the sky and killed his sheep and servants: "God where are you?" The Chaldeans stole his camels and killed his servants: "God where are you?" Then a great wind destroyed his oldest son's house, killing all of his children: "God where are you?" Afflicted with painful boils: "God where are you?" His wife tells him to "curse God, and die" (2:9). "God where are you?"

But God was *not* absent. God was preparing to reveal more of himself than Job had ever experienced before. Never forget—*there is always more of God than we can see!*

What Job did not know, what he could not know, except by way of faith, was that his boils would be healed, his herds would be doubled, and seven more sons and three more daughters would be born to him, the fairest in the land!

And these things were restored to him because in the midst of his darkness, in the midst of his pain and suffering, in the midst of all his unanswered questions Job still reached out to God and cried: "I know that my redeemer lives, and that he shall stand at the latter day upon the earth; And . . . in my flesh shall I see God: Whom I shall see for myself, and my eyes shall behold" (19:25–27).

Like Job, Horatio G. Spafford certainly knew what it was like to hold tightly to the Lord even through the valley of the shadow of death—times *four!* In 1873, after hearing that his wife had been "saved alone" in a terrible accident at sea and that all four of his daughters had perished (think of it!) he quickly set sail to join her. Halfway across the great Atlantic, in the general vicinity of the previous tragedy, he looked out over the side of the ship into the deep, dark waters that had claimed his children and penned:

> When peace, like a river, attendeth my way,
>> When sorrows like sea billows roll;
> Whatever my lot, Thou hast taught me to say,
>> It is well, it is well with my soul.

Heaven alone knows the millions that have been touched and comforted by those words through the decades. But only recently has another stanza, mostly forgotten, been recovered. While writing this book I came across the original fourth of his six verses:

> For me, be it Christ, be it Christ hence to live:
>> If Jordan above me shall roll,
> No pang shall be mine, for in death as in life
>> Thou wilt whisper Thy peace to my soul.[4]

The Lord is longing to whisper peace to you as well. To develop something awesome within you, but that will never happen as long as your eyes are only on the gloom of your unspeakable loss. The secret is to begin to look inward and to ask the Father to show you what he wants you to learn *and* what changes he desires to make within you. To cling to him, even when you may not feel him.

Luke 2:51 describes how Jesus lived in submission to his parents: "And he went down with them, and came to Nazareth, and was subject unto them." Deity did not eclipse humanity so as to make learning unnecessary. Even Jesus experienced the discipline

4. Spafford, "It Is Well with My Soul," (1873, public domain).

and submission that accompanies learning. What is it that God wants you to learn? What is it that he desires to form within you? What greater purpose is he trying to develop within you?

Friend, your heavenly Father wants to use you in wonderful ways in the next chapter of your life. Don't despise the loneliness of your unspeakable loss, but learn to embrace it and glean from it and understand that the Lord of the harvest has wonderful reasons for allowing you the privilege of walking through such a place. He *will* use you and he will decide when and where that will be.

"But, how long will I be in this place?" I don't know—but God does and he does all things well! And when it is over, you will know the sweetness of life that only comes to those who have emerged victorious from a place of refuge and pain, a place of retreat and sorrow, a place where he gives songs in the night!

Psalm 34:4–8: "I sought the Lord, and he heard me, and delivered me from all my fears. . . . This poor man cried, and the Lord heard him, and saved him out of all his troubles. Oh, taste and see that the Lord is good: blessed is the man who trusts in him."

ψ

While serving as missionaries in West Africa, my wife and I and three of our four children were returning home from dinner on a beautiful May evening in 2001. Suddenly, we came upon a terrible, horrific accident that had just happened seconds earlier. A taxi was being pushed by three young men, probably teens, and the driver when it was struck from behind by a large bus. The impact had sent the taxi another fifty or sixty yards down the road leaving the three boys lying in its wake and the driver in the sandy berm to our right. We stopped our SUV just in front of them and Paulette positioned it to keep other cars from hitting them as well as to provide some light upon the injured while my oldest son Lucas, just four days past his seventeenth birthday, and I jumped out to assist. Our two youngest (twelve and eight) stayed in the car and prayed with mom.

Very few locals know what to do in situations like that aside from call for the ambulance and wait. While not medical professionals ourselves, unfortunately, this was not the first time we had encountered something of this nature, although this one certainly was the worst. More broken glass and debris than I remember seeing before, with bodies lying broken and bleeding and dying on the four-lane highway. Perhaps some were already dead.

As the first upon the scene my first thought was to try and assess the injuries and to stop any severe bleeding. The first two young men that I came to both had serious head wounds. I immediately peeled off my dress shirt to use as a compress to stop the bleeding as well as keep the sand, dirt, and broken glass at bay and provide some modest comfort compared to the hard pavement.

Each was someone's son. I spoke to him in his tribal language and asked his name. He responded "Ibrahima (Abraham)." Probably about the same age as Luke. By the grace of God, my son was and is safe, healthy, and whole—and after that night has given me even more reason to be proud to call him my son.

Initially, I had jumped out of the car (alone, or so I thought) and ran ahead to the injured boys. As I knelt there and placed my shirt on the wounds and wiped blood on his head and face, it was then that I realized that Luke had followed me out of the car and was now kneeling, shirtless like his dad, at the boy's legs and had laid his hands on him and had begun praying for him.

For the next forty-five minutes we moved among the three worst injured of the four (no one else would touch them), walking up and down the road, kneeling to adjust our makeshift compresses, which consisted only of my shirt and some long sheets of white paper that someone had thrown our way, trying to abate more bleeding than I had ever before witnessed in person. We went from one to the other speaking words of comfort in French, English, and the very few tribal words that we knew, trying to keep them alert and not drifting into shock, praying here, adjusting there, not sure if some were even dead or alive. The one who was lying further up the road had a deep cut on his leg that was life-threatening. We tried to explain in French to the bystanders that he needed to be turned over and a compress applied to his thigh or he would bleed to death. We weren't even sure at the time if he was still alive, so profuse was the bleeding under his leg.

Eventually another man came and immediately comprehended what we were trying to accomplish, ripped off a piece of the injured man's T-shirt, and applied a tourniquet. We moved back and forth between the three. Sometimes Luke was with me, sometimes he was doing something else. Once or twice early on I looked across the body at him and reminded him to be careful about not getting any blood on any open cuts he might have, but other than normal precautions such as that, we tried to stop the bleeding, keep the wounds covered, and speak words of hope to the injured. *If we Christians are afraid to touch the bleeding and dying then they will not be touched! If Mark 16:18 is not for situations such as this, then what is it for?!*

Out of the hundreds who had gathered, only one or two said anything to those on the ground. Luke and I would kneel down by them, pray over them, call them by name, tell them to stay awake, tell them to have courage, and the like. Other than that, there was nothing we could do but wait for the ambulance to arrive.

After about forty-five minutes, the injured had been taken away, the police were directing traffic, and after a few farewells and "thank-yous" to some who had helped us, we kicked the largest pieces of glass and debris off of the road, and headed back to the car to resume our journey home. Of course, Paulette and our youngest two all had shed many, many tears as they sat in the car watching and praying.

After arriving home, we scrubbed up with soap, alcohol, etc., and finally had time to let our minds relax a bit and decipher what had just transpired. As I stood in the living room, Lucas walked in and said something that perhaps eclipsed even his own actions of prayer earlier in the evening. He said, "You know Dad, maybe traveling out to a village and preaching and things like that aren't the most important things we can do as missionaries. Oh, not that they aren't important, because they are, but *maybe just being available for the spontaneous things like tonight is just as important, too."*

His three siblings looked up at us from the couch. I thought a minute and then added, "I think you're right, Luke. Because those people out there tonight will not soon forget the sight of two shirtless white guys running around in the middle of all that blood and all that mess. They won't forget that we reached down and touched those who lay on the ground with such severe injuries and the fact that we talked to them and tried to calm them. We tried to let the love of Christ flow out from our lives to hundreds of passersby *who didn't even know what it was.* But maybe someday twenty or forty years from now, they will hear something that will cause them to remember and perhaps they will say, 'That's what those two guys were doing that night!'"

"You see," I went on to explain to my kids, "the Bible says some plant, some water, some gather in the fruit, but each one plays a part. We didn't give an altar call tonight, but maybe we did give the introduction to the sermon and someone else will water after us."

Injured friend, trying to make sense of the ashes of yesterday's dreams, you, too, have wounded and dying all around you every day! You, too, may seem overwhelmed, perhaps even alone and afraid! But simply "be available" to them even in the midst of your own brokenness. Especially in the midst of your own brokenness. Be present to touch them and encourage them and sooth their fears and pray for them and God will add the increase, he will do the rest.

If we will be available. Even in the midst of our own wreckage and debris, our own horrific tragedy, our own injury and pain. You are preaching a beautiful message—right there in the middle of your unspeakable loss.

And like Lazarus of old (John 11) God will ultimately bring resurrection to your loss. Only Christ can turn death into life, defeat into victory, and mourning into joy! You may not feel him at this moment—but he is near! You may not be aware of him just yet—but he is right on time! You may not know where he is in the middle of your hurt and disappointment—but he *does* care and he is about to reveal himself as your personal life-giver!

Soon you shall sing with Job, "He knows the way that I take: when he has tried me, I shall come forth as gold. . . . Though he slay me, yet will I trust in him" (23:10; 13:15).

And when he reveals his resurrection power you will rejoice with exceeding joy. Where is God when it hurts? Where is he when all around you are the reminders of what you once had, but have no more? Where is he in the midst of your personal tomb of despair wondering why he is so painfully silent? *Silent!* Where is he? He is present! And that is enough.

The Christ of John's gospel speaks into four days of silence and a corpse begins to quiver! He dictates to decay and fingers of death loose their icy grip! He cries out to the lifeless and man becomes a living soul! He shouts into a tomb and a body stands to its feet! He calls to him and calls him by name and Lazarus emerges from the grave and rejoins the land of the living! He is and always will be the revealer of resurrection power!

And what he did for Lazarus yesterday he will do for you today! Listen closely. Can you hear him? Do you hear him calling— to *you!* Calling you to lay aside graveclothes of pain and heartache and stand to your feet. Calling you to let go of yesterday's wounds and to experience true freedom in your life. Calling you to remove the facial cloth of depression and despair in order to inhale the freshness and fullness of his Holy Spirit. Calling you to come forth from your tomb of grief, to come forth from the darkness of your misery and enter into the power of his resurrection life! Calling you to fully learn of

The simple power of a broken life.

This was the key to Job's restoration. He held deeply within his soul an unshakeable belief in God. Yes, it was at times mixed with doubt and wrapped in mystery. Just as life occasionally is for all of us. Yes, out of his anguish and grief he said some things he should not have said. Yes, he ended up being rebuked by God. No, he didn't get it perfect. But all things considered, he came close. For one of God's children two thousand years *before* the revelation of Jesus and the illumination of the Holy Spirit, he came real close. May his example serve to help you in your valley of brokenness and may it lead you in simplicity and power to the sweetness of the Father's restoration as well.

5

The Pain of Seedless Ache

—HANNAH

> Prayer is not asking. Prayer is putting oneself in the hands
> of God, at His disposition,
>
> and listening to His voice in the depth of our hearts.
>
> When you don't have anything, then you have everything.
>
> —MOTHER TERESA, *ESSENTIAL WRITINGS*

IS THERE ANYTHING SO powerfully felt, yet so hard to describe as the pain of stolen or unfulfilled dreams, hopes, or loves? The pain of seedless ache is simultaneously straightforward in its simplicity, while at the same time soul-crushing in its profundity.

The barren womb. The unmatched longings of singleness. The aspiration that never seems to take root. The disappointments of middle-aged life, the regrets of still older life. The healing that has not yet come. The loneliness that has.

Hannah emerges from the pages of the Old Testament with a distress of soul that is instantly felt by anyone who has ever known the bitter dread of watching the years pass by while their situation remains unchanged. Unable to conceive and mocked mercilessly by the other wife in a polygamous household the ache of her barrenness finally reached the breaking point. First Samuel 1:6, 7 records: "And her adversary also provoked her relentlessly . . . therefore she wept, and did not eat." Verse 10 adds: "And she was in bitterness of soul, and prayed unto the Lord, and wept greatly."

So intense was her pain that as she poured out her heart to God in prayer the prophet observing her unintelligible grief thought that she was drunk! And the people who misread your predicament and undervalue the depth of your agony are equally shortsighted when they offer up their pitiful platitudes of compassionless comfort.

She wasn't drunk, she was *broken!* She wasn't numb from alcohol, she was numb from life! She wasn't full of wine, she was empty of child!

The pain of barrenness is severe in its own right, but to then be misunderstood and self-righteously rebuked only adds to the silent, searing ache within. Oh, how Hannah must have longed for someone to understand the depths of her anguish! How her soul must have craved relief from the seedless ache within!

That's the funny thing about pain. You don't appreciate it in its *fullest* until it rages at its *fiercest*, thereby leaving you with the *least* capability to fight it.

The prophet Isaiah described Jesus as a "man of sorrows, acquainted with grief" (Isa 53:3). Sorrow and grief will sometimes be experienced by the child of God! Ours is not a world without pain. Rather, it is a world of victory in spite of pain and sorrow and the promise of a new world to come! The cup which the Father extends for you to drink is sometimes a cup of sorrow. A bitter cup of unfulfilled emptiness. George MacDonald imparts: "The Son of God . . . suffered unto the death, not that men might not suffer, but that their suffering might be like his."[1]

Unknown to anyone, save the mind of God in the annals of his majestic, mysterious sovereignty, he sometimes allows a painful cup of seedless ache to be lifted to our lips. Some would curse the cup away. Some would confess the cup away. Some would politely refuse it, hoping their denial would change things and perhaps even be seen as spiritual. But the balance of Scripture reveals

1. MacDonald, *Unspoken Sermons*, 30.

to us yet another alternative—that of sweet resignation to higher purposes that we know not of.

Yes, there is a time to rebuke the enemy and all that emits from his foul existence. Yes, there is a time to stand strong on the word of God and boldly confess his promises. Yes, there is a time to draw a line in the sand against untoward circumstances of life and declare, "No more! Not here, not today, not *ever!*" And there is also a time—a blessed and glorious time—to embrace the pain of seedless ache and learn from its shadowy pangs. A time to receive the peace that passes all human understanding. Glorious, deliberate resignation to the perfection of his divine will—no higher form of faith than this!

What comfort we find in Psalm 34:18: "The Lord is near unto them that are of a broken heart; and saves such as are of a contrite spirit." One of the marvelous qualities of God is his perfect timing. He is never late and he is never too early. He is always on time. Even when it seems that he is nowhere to be found.

Our starting point in finding God in the midst of our ache is always here—in surrender to his will and his timing. Friend, please learn the refreshing joy of surrender to divine, deliberate delay! Even in the darkest hours—wait on him.

Ask any musician, ask any athlete—timing is everything. Selfish pity will always occlude full surrender. There can be one or the other—but never both.

If you are hurting, take a deep breath, stop your mind from reeling, and strengthen yourself with Isaiah 40:31: "They that wait upon the Lord shall renew their strength; they shall mount up with wings like eagles; they shall run, and not be weary; and they shall walk, and not faint." You *must* understand this. And you *must* accept this, or you will never grow into a greater knowledge of God and his ways.

Several years ago one author put it this way: "Our wills must be broken to His will. To be broken is the beginning of revival. It is painful, it is humiliating, it is the only way. It is being 'Not I, but Christ,' and a 'C' is a bent 'I.'"[2]

2. Hession, *Calvary Road*, 21–22.

When the scope of your personal ache seems overwhelming you must resist the temptation to fill that ache with the anesthetizing effect of other things. Knowing Jesus Christ as your personal Lord and Savior is the most thrilling, exhilarating thing you can do in this life. The problem is the enemy fights us hard along this line and tries to convince us that the opposite is true.

Satan wants us to believe that serving him is thrilling—but service to God is dull and boring. He wants us to believe that he has all the good ideas, all the good times, and all the good fun—and that Christ really has nothing to offer. The devil would like for you to succumb to a mindset that walking in holiness and righteousness is old fashioned, out of date, and irrelevant and that being a follower of Jesus is dry and mundane. Of course, both the word of God and life itself prove that not to be true. But the temptation is there, just the same.

During those difficult times when your heart is yearning for some glimpse of that which will be, but as of yet remains achingly absent, you must commit that you will walk in obedience to the light which you do possess. Even when your footsteps are deadened by the passing of time and the weight of unrealized dreams.

You are not accountable for someone else's light, you are not accountable for light which you do not have, you are not accountable for the light which may come tomorrow, but you must absolutely walk in obedience to the light which you do possess today. It may seem to be but a single flicker. It may appear to be misty and foggy all around. But walk with the light which you *do* possess.

If God has spoken a certain word to you, then you must walk according to the light of that word. If he has placed a specific burden for something within your heart, then you must walk according to the light of that burden. If he has told you what your attitude must be then you must respond with the grace that love requires—even from the barrenness of your unfulfilled present.

This is a great proving ground! You may not understand all of his mysterious purposes and ways, but stop cursing the darkness of your barren existence, believe that your ache will one day be made whole and begin to walk in obedience to the light which you do possess! Don't give up—trust him! He is there!

Former secretary of state Condoleezza Rice refers to such times as "the privilege of struggle" and observes: "Struggle and sorrow are not license to give way to self-doubt, self-pity, and defeat but are an opportunity to find a renewed spirit and strength to carry on."[3]

May I ask you plainly? In the pain and discontent of your present season are you practicing faithfulness even in the small things? Are you faithful with your tithe, which by the way belongs to your local church? Rest assured one of the first invitations you will receive during a season of barrenness is the invitation to compromise your tithing.

Are you faithful with your time? What areas of ministry are you involved in? I did not ask you what great revelation you have in your future. I asked you, what are you doing for the kingdom of God right now? Right now!

Are you faithful with Bible study and prayer? If you are not careful, the pain and sense of abandonment during your unfulfilled days, your seedless days will lead you to a dead end of darkness and self-doubt. The ache of barrenness will consume spiritual disciplines in a moment, before you even have time to notice they are gone.

Are you faithful to gather with brothers and sisters for worship? The principle of the fourth commandment has never been rescinded—"Remember the Sabbath day, to keep it holy" (Exod 20:8). Don't let the enemy isolate you. Danger! Danger! Danger!

Are you faithful with your emotions? The weight and desperation of your situation can so easily lead to fatigue and discouragement. However, you are still in control of your emotions. Will you allow yourself to wallow in the recesses of depression, pity, and blame or will you be faithful with your emotions, seeing that they glorify God? One author adds: "Discouragement is that little voice on your shoulder, whispering in your ear that all your hopes and aspirations are nothing more than youthful naïvety. There is no

---

3. Montgomery, *Were It Not for Grace*, 5.

point persevering. How corrosive that little voice is; how ruinous to gospel zeal and drive!"[4]

Are you faithful with your attitude? Oh, you may hold your tongue, but what are you thinking on the inside?!

Sometimes I have seen individuals back off in their relationship with Christ over a period of time. They gradually begin to become less passionate, resulting in a stirring, a restlessness in their spirit which they often wrongly interpret as "something must be wrong with the pastor" or "something must be wrong with the church." In fact, it is a result of their own gradual slide into lukewarm-ness. Don't allow your discontent to lead you into poor decisions. Look to Jesus, not others!

So often, as Bevere conveys, "we've undersold the grace of God. We've declared rightly that it saves, forgives, and is a free gift of His love. However, we've not declared that it has changed our very nature and empowers us to not live as we used to. We've avoided telling people that they're now empowered to forsake ungodly behavior. The result of such silence is that believers are ignorant of godliness and *missing out on God's presence*."[5] Coolness in our relationship with Jesus must lead us *to* him, not *away* from his presence. Restlessness should awaken greater passion and deeper hunger for God. Discontent must fasten us more tightly to the cross that is our glory—even when the pain of seedless ache seems to convince us that our season is far passed.

Every one of us has faced or will face difficult, dark, and mysterious things in life for which we have no solution and no answer. Sometimes these things are so painful and hit us with such ferocity out of the blue that we don't even have a response! We simply do not know what to say. In those barren times, in those seasons of seedless ache, Romans 8:28 is the anchor in the midst of the storm: "And we know that all things work together for good to them who love God, to them who are the called according to his purpose." The Contemporary English Version reads: "We know that God is always at work for the good of everyone who loves him."

4. Ash, *Zeal without Burnout*, 96.

5. Bevere, *Good or God?*, 152 (emphasis mine).

When what we long for, ache for, never seems to come to pass, we develop a sense of grief not unlike that felt through the passing of a friend or family member, the closing of a business or plant or church, the dream that is nowhere to be found on reality's horizon. Grief is pain from a loss, a journey, a process, a sense of sadness due to a loss. All grief is not the same! But God is always there in the midst of our pain bringing good out of the grief, bringing help out of the hurt, wholeness out of the wound. As a dear friend of mine, elder brother in the faith, and pastor to thousands, Bishop David L. Thomas, once confided: "When you ask the Lord, 'Show me your mind, show me your heart,' anticipate pain, anticipate hurt, anticipate brokenness."[6]

At times we must know even when we cannot feel! At times you may not be able to see the path God has for you. You may not be able to see where you are going—but don't miss this: *not knowing where you are going does not mean you are going nowhere!* He has promised to work it out in the mysterious times! *"All things work together for good . . ."* We are the called and the called do not give up! He will work it out!

Oh, friend! Aching so deeply from the unanswered prayer down inside of you. You may feel down and discouraged, left out and lonely; it may seem the battle is over, the war is lost; you may think that defeat is your destiny and losing is your lot; but you are the called—something heroic is about to be birthed in you! He will work it out! You see, God uses circumstances to get *out of* us what is *in* us! Even when we cannot see what that may be.

We like the purpose of God but not always the process. But we must go through the process before the purpose. Why? Because

---

6. David L. Thomas is bishop of Victory Christian Center in Youngstown, Ohio, a multisite, multicultural mega church with eight campuses and over five thousand people. Beyond that, he founded and leads Next Level Leadership Network, an international organization spanning denominations that includes churches, missions organizations, and ministers. He is also president and founder of Legacy, A Global Kingdom Alliance, which is a network of networks that promotes connecting the generations through Launching, Living, and Leaving a Legacy. Bishop Thomas is also a founding member of the John Maxwell Team.

there is power in the process! I have known dark, painful, mysterious seasons just like you. Some of my own making, some from the hands of others. And I can tell you from personal experience that *growing closer to Jesus and becoming more like him is the sweetest, most satisfying experience you will ever know!* Other things may shine for a moment, but nothing compares to the depth and reality of knowing Jesus. Really, truly, deeply knowing him.

There is a sweet, sweet point of surrender where we know that in spite of our imperfections, failures and humanness—we are closer to the heart of God than we ever have been before. And that, dear friends, is worth more than all the treasures the world can offer. I know you are hurting right now, but he will work it out! *All* things. *Painful* things. *Your* things.

Commit to faithfulness—even in the small things! May the Lord find in you a commitment and steadfastness of purpose that will assist you and bless you as you walk through your days of seedless ache. It is the discipline of faithfulness in small things that will serve you well. The discipline of steadfastness—even in the seemingly insignificant things. The discipline of being true in every area that the Holy Spirit is whispering to you about. Your season of seeming non-productivity will not last forever. Your Samuel will come! Until he does, take courage from Psalm 34:7, "The angel of the Lord encamps round about those who fear him, and delivers them."

God answered Hannah's prayer and blessed her with a son, Samuel. From the pain of her seedless ache a prayer was born. From that prayer a prophet was born. And from the life of that prophet one of the great leaders of Israel was born. Samuel. One of the larger-than-life giants of the faith! From a humble woman who felt like her prayer would never be answered and that tomorrow would never come.

Just like you. Right now. Right there.

Hannah knew full well that God knows the real value of what has been discarded, tossed aside, and thrown away. In her song of praise she testified, "He raises up the poor out of the dust and lifts up the beggar from the refuse, to set them among princes, and to make them inherit the throne of glory" (1 Sam 2:8).

He will be glorified in your life as well! He will raise you up and honor you—*you!* He will answer your prayer of desperation as he did for Hannah—*if*—you do not exit your ache prematurely.

James 1:4 addresses our need to patiently wait for the will of God to be revealed: "But let patience have her perfect work, that you may be perfect and entire, lacking nothing." Please be certain of this. If we move from a place of service or vocation or calling prematurely we will find it extremely difficult, if not impossible, to remove the frustration that caused the move in the first place. We *must* persevere through the dry, difficult desert times until a greater understanding of God's plan is revealed.

It is crucial that you step *to* something and not merely *away* from something. I am referring to dreams, ambitions, and finding the will of God. There may be rare—very rare—instances where the Lord leads you to take a step of faith and leave a current position or assignment or locale before he begins to show you the next step, but such occurrences are not the norm for our day-to-day living and should *never* be made out of emotion alone. Especially if that emotion is anger. Getting mad at your boss, telling him off, storming out and driving home only to tell your wife and friends "God led me to take a step of faith" is at once silly, shallow, and quite presumptuous.

Most of the time—in fact, the vast majority of the time—the Lord will first begin to speak to you about change. He will then begin to bring confirming words and signs to pass. And as you begin to mentally engage with the possibility of change he will start to prompt you toward something else.

Oh, to be quite sure you may only receive the faintest glimpse of what he is about to do, but it will be marked by peace. It will have the kiss of grace upon it. It may be a bit (or a lot!) frightening as well, but there will be a sense that "God is in this" even when his way is mysterious.

And in the meantime, when the pain of seedless ache reminds you that your longing has not yet been realized, stay true to your compass, true to your integrity, and true to your God. The *simple* power of a broken life. *Simple*. Not easy. Not pain-free. But the simplicity that is found in Jesus and patiently waiting on him.

6

The Pain of Betrayal and False Accusation

—DAVID

> As far as David's having authority: Men who don't have
> it talk about it all the time. Submit, submit, that's all you
> hear. David had authority, but I don't think that fact ever
> occurred to him! We were 600 no-goods with a leader who
> cried a lot. That's all we were!
>
> —GENE EDWARDS, *A TALE OF THREE KINGS*

IT WILL ALWAYS BE remembered as one of the greatest victories
in military history. That hot, impossible day when a young man,
probably still in his teens, strode out to meet the enemy who
instilled sheer fright and panic into the seasoned soldiers of the
Israeli army.

Before Jonathan Netanyahu. Before David Ben-Gurion. Before the tragic heroes of Masada there was . . . the boy. The here-
tofore insignificant shepherd boy. The youngest of eight boys. The
errand boy who was absolutely confounded as to why no one—not
one!—would stand up for God and his people and face that blas-
phemous agitator of everything righteous.

David was concerned neither with the height of the arrogant
challenger nor the length of his spear. This was God's battle and
God's name and God's honor were at stake. What was nine and a
half feet to the Creator of the universe!

He did it for his God, saying, in essence: "Who are you to defy the Lord God?" (1 Sam 17:45). He did it for his people. He did it for his king. Because true leaders don't run away from problems. David ran *toward* Goliath! Everyone else thought Goliath was too big to fight. David thought, with God's help, Goliath was too big to miss!

ψ

One who endeavors to live a life of brokenness before the Lord will repeatedly be given opportunities to discover fresh dependency on the Lord Jesus. The pain of false accusation is often presented to us as just such an opportunity. And so it was with the future king, who first had to learn what it is to be harassed by hounds, cursed by a king who was mad, and comforted in a cave of icy silence. But in such a cave you will find a faith that you cannot find anywhere else.

Who can fully know and understand the confluence of circumstances, emotions, and fears that drove a heroic king to madness? Saul allowed resentment, jealousy, and hatred to boil within until those things gave way to tormenting evil spirits. Be careful what you allow to breed inside your spirit! The road of resentment will always lead to a bitter end.

David had been nothing but loyal and supportive of Saul. Indeed, David would exercise majestic restraint in submission to "the Lord's anointed," repeatedly refusing to harm him or move against Saul's position as king.

And what of your Saul? What of that individual's unfounded accusations against you? What of the betrayal that has arisen suddenly and unexpectedly, landing with a sharp thud in the wall next to your head? Where did *that* come from? And why? Yes, *why?*

Gene Edwards stirs us with this dramatic insight from his classic work *A Tale of Three Kings*:

> God has *His* eyes fastened sharply on another King Saul.
> Not the visible one standing up there throwing spears at

you. No, God is looking at *another* King Saul. One just as bad—or worse.

God is looking at the King Saul in *you*. . . .

He breathes in the lungs and beats in the breast of all of us. There is only one way to get rid of him. He must be annihilated. . . . David the sheepherder would have grown up to become King Saul II, except that God cut away the Saul inside David's heart. The operation, by the way, took years and was a brutalizing experience that almost killed the patient. And what were the scalpel and tongs God used to remove this inner Saul?

God used the outer Saul. . . . David accepted this fate. He embraced the cruel circumstances. He lifted no hand, nor offered resistance. Nor did he grandstand his piety. Silently, privately, he bore the crucibles. Because of this he was deeply wounded. His whole inner being was mutilated. His personality was altered. When the gore was over, David was barely recognizable.[1]

I once heard that amazing psalmist and anointed preacher Bishop Joseph Garlington opine in his delightfully unique way: "Heroes aren't born, they're cornered." Ah. So true! Is there some hero about to emerge from the situation that even now has you cornered? Yes, *you!* The fact that your back is up against the wall does not mean that you are defeated. It may simply mean that a hero is about to be born!

Like David, we must remain firm in our commitment to Christ-likeness no matter the discomfort or pain. Inner transformation becomes immensely more important than whether or not you carry the day. Being more like Christ is more important than being "right." Being more like him is all that matters! Remember, David lived in a cave of brokenness before he ruled the people.

Perhaps, like David, you find yourself falsely blamed, suffering for things that are not your fault. Is there some unjust accusation that has risen against you? Has God called you to some task, but before you inherit your throne he has allowed a divine interlude of testing and preparation? Do you secretly long for a greater revelation of the

---

1. Edwards, *Tale of Three Kings*, 21–23.

Lord and a deeper understanding of his ways, yet the way is dark, cold, mysterious, and void of fulfillment?

The false accusations of a deranged king resulted in David spending time on the run, living off the land, hiding out in caves. Speaking of caves, can there be any more depressing and lonely place than a cave? Dark. Damp. Cold. Musty. Claustrophobic. Not meant for human habitation—especially a human with a shepherd's love of the open fields! Yet, is it not in the close confines of the cave that we discover that it is the trials which make the victories so glorious? The rain which makes the sunshine so brilliant? The pain which makes the healing so wonderful? The desert which makes the flowing river so sweet? And the gloom of the cave which makes the light of his face so precious?

During one such season of seclusion David wrote the Fifty-Seventh Psalm: "Be merciful to me, O God, be merciful to me! For my soul trusts in you; And in the shadow of Your wings I will make my refuge, until these calamities have passed by" (NKJV). Did you catch that? "In the shadow of Your wings I will make my refuge." While such imagery certainly alludes to the love and protection given by God to those who are his, it also may speak of the wings of the Cherubim that overlooked the mercy seat on the ark of the covenant.

Here is the key: *David wanted to be as close as possible to the presence of the Lord!* What do you strive to be close to? What passion burns within your heart? Jeremiah, himself no stranger to pain, rejection, and heartache, reflected in Lamentations 3:22–23 "Through the Lord's mercies we are not consumed, because His compassions fail not. They are new every morning; Great is Your faithfulness" (NKJV).

Years later when David fled from the advancing armies of his own son's rebellion, he cried out in distress: "Lord, how are they increased that trouble me! Many are they that rise up against me. Many there are who say of my soul, There is no help for him in God" (Ps 3:1–2).

Is this not the cry of your heart today? Alcohol and drugs trouble you, rise up against you, and sneer, "There is no help in God!"

False accusers and the poisoned arrows of gossip and innuendo mockingly pronounce, "There is no help for her in God!" Financial difficulty and looming unemployment trouble you, rise up against you, and declare, "There is no help for him in God!" From the secret recesses of the history of your life past sins and former failures assert, "There is no help for him in God!" Depressive thoughts, addictive behaviors, cutting, purging, and a hundred other voices insidiously avow, "There is no help for her in God!"

But what all of these have forgotten is that the cave may be lonely—but we are not alone! The cave may be dark—and yet there is a light! Cool may be its air—yet there is a familiar and soothing warmth. For standing guard at the entrance of your cave is one who is the Captain of the cave!

God's plan for your life is that you will emerge in victory—victory!—from your cave of betrayal and false accusation. That you would not only stand in victory, but that you would use your story to lead others to their victory as well. Phillip Keller points out that "amid his grief, amid his exile, amid his rebel comrades David was learning first-hand the frustration and anguish of the oppressed. He would develop an enormous empathy for the underprivileged of his people. Never would he be immune to the suffering of his subjects when in due time he became their monarch."[2]

ψ

Betrayal. False accusation. Was the life of King David ever any darker than when his own son, his own flesh and blood attempted to seize the throne and the aged ruler found himself on the run once again?

Some might say, "David, where is your God?" Others might mock, "David, have you no faith?" But David knew God was preparing to reveal his blessing, his favor, in his time and in his way. That is why he could sing through tear filled eyes as he fled Jerusalem the rest of the Third Psalm: "But you, O Lord, are a shield for me; my glory, and the lifter up of my head." He sang: "I cried unto

---

2. Keller, *David: Saul's Tyranny*, 121.

THE SIMPLE POWER OF A BROKEN LIFE

the Lord with my voice, and he heard me out of his holy hill. I lay down and slept; I awaked; for the Lord sustained me. I will not be afraid of ten thousands of people, who have set themselves against me round about [because] Salvation belongs unto the Lord; your blessing is upon your people" (Ps 3:3–6, 8). He is the Captain of your cave! Whether your betrayal happened in the throne room (market place) or in the home he is still your Captain—even in the darkest, most painful of caves.

When on the end of unfounded criticism or false accusation, never forget, *evil is a stream which one day flows back to its source!* Do not take things into your own hands. Never, ever, *ever* seek to retaliate in the flesh.

The common assumption is that a meek person is one who is timid and cannot help themselves. But scriptural meekness has to do with power and the ability to control that power. It is the opposite of self-assertiveness. Meekness is not occupied with self at all. It has been said that *meekness is velvet-covered steel.*

The insane king hunted David, and David more than once had Saul within his power. Likewise, your enemies may place obstacles before you in the ordinary course of day-to-day affairs—but you have power over them! The power of attitude, the power of disposition, the power of your tongue, the power of blessing, the power of faith!

The wicked may devise their schemes and enact their plans—but you have power to pray, power to persevere, and power to prevail.

God is able to turn the plans of your enemies upon their own heads. Your responsibility is to sit down in the mouth of your cave of despair, ponder the gracious protection of your Shepherd King, and sing your song of deliverance!

Please understand, in your cave of isolation and rejection, in your own personal Adullam, not all traps are intentional! David refers to the fact that his enemies had "prepared a net" and "dug a pit" for him. Some of the traps that you will face in your cave are not just the ones that have been intentionally set for you, but you will also face emotional and attitudinal traps that will equally defeat God's purpose for your life. Not all traps are intentionally set by those who oppose you. Some spring from within and some are activated by well-meaning supporters!

You must beware of traps of self-pity, traps of bitterness, negativity, criticism, and complaint. Here's the danger—these traps are set by those who call themselves your friends!

In your cave, in your season of pain, be very careful about those whom you allow to speak into your life! The timeless truth that we all understand, yet so many find difficult to live is this: *you will become the people you associate with*. Let that resonate within your mind for a moment. Now repeat it to yourself slowly, deliberately, and thoughtfully: *I will become the people I associate with. I will become the people I associate with.*

Powerful, isn't it? That is why it is so important to surround yourself with good people. It is absolutely critical to your spiritual well-being to associate with those who are positive and strong in faith.

Personally, I do not have any close friends or associates in my life who are negative, cynical, critical people. I can love people like that; I want to help people like that; I pray for people like that; I will shepherd people like that, but I will not allow them to be intimately connected to my life because negative, critical, cynical people suck the life and the joy out of everyone and everything they come in contact with!

And if you watch their lives over a period of time you will see that turmoil and strife always follow them wherever they go and whatever they do. That is because turmoil and strife always follow crisis-oriented people. That bears repeating: *turmoil and strife always follow crisis-oriented people.* You don't really want more of that in your life, do you?

Now, I know what some of you are thinking. You allow these people into your lives because you think you can overlook their faults. But I promise you, they will adversely affect your spiritual walk to a greater degree than you can ever imagine.

Some of you are saying, and I hear this all the time as a pastor, "Well, I don't necessarily agree with what they are saying, but

I just want to listen. They called and I did not want to be rude, etc. After all, don't my positive words have greater power than their negative words?"

Yes, but here it is: While it is true that positive words have greater force than negative words, *negative words have greater power than neutral words!* And that is the danger of listening to negative, critical people. Unless you are speaking more positive than their negative, unless you are speaking more life than their death, your words are neutral and their words will impact you and suck you down into the dysfunctional vortex of their own bitterness and negativity. The New Living Translation of Proverbs 16:27–28 reads: "Scoundrels create trouble; their words are a destructive blaze. A troublemaker plants seeds of strife; gossip separates the best of friends."

As you walk through a season of betrayal and false accusation never forget—his grace is sufficient! The enemy will come against you with horrific force while you are in your season of isolation. It is then that you must remember the goodness and the grace of your heavenly Father.

David had nothing to produce of his own merit—he was in a barren cave! He had nothing that he could muster in his own strength that would have produced the same results as Jehovah. Nothing of his own talent and ability that would change the heart of this mad king who sought his life. Nothing—except the awesome grace of an amazing God.

Please understand this: your healing and your restoration will always commence with the proper perspective! If your eyes are only on the vastness of your problem or the depth of your pain then you must change your focus! You must lift up your head, you must look higher than the towering walls of the enemy's fortress, higher than the dark storm clouds of fear and confusion, higher than the endless horizon of obstacles and affliction.

You must lift up your head and see heaven! See the throne! See the One who created the heavens and the earth and from whose hand all things have been made! You are not without hope! The word of God declares: "He heals the brokenhearted and bandages their wounds" (Ps 147:3 NLT). Trust God to put you back together again. *He has not broken you to crush you or destroy you, but to enlarge your capacity to be useful.*

One of the challenges a cave presents us with is isolation. And sometimes the isolation we face is due to our own self-imposed exile. We have been wounded, so we retreat. We have been injured by the spurious spear of false accusation, so we close off. Some would-be ruler has hurled unjust slander our way, so we escape to a less vulnerable abode.

But great caution must be taken when we back off into a safer place. There is nothing wrong for escaping to gather ourselves and be refreshed. The danger lies in allowing that temporary retreat from others to turn into a self-imposed exile that shuts out the world and all who dwell therein.

Anne Graham Lotz cautions: "Self-imposed exile can become a prison cell that locks from the inside. . . . The key that works is to cry out to God in humility and sincerity. . . . We have to deny our pride. We have to want to come out of exile into the glory of His presence more than we want to remain where we are. . . . If you say *no* then your stubbornness must be applauded in hell. Your silence must be deafening in Heaven. And surely, as God opens His mouth to speak to you, there must be tears on His face."[3]

ψ

Another truth that emerges from our cave of betrayal is the simple fact that one of the greatest pains we will face in life is the pain of transition. And often such transition is brought about by betrayal or false accusation.

Even in the minefield of false accusation there may be things that do contain nuggets of truth from which we must learn. How crucial it is to be able to discard the 90 percent and learn from the 10 percent that may be true. This is a great secret to spiritual success! When the world falls apart, we have to ask, "Is it me? What part did I play?" and then walk in obedience to what the Lord reveals.

3. Lotz, *Wounded by God's People*, 169–70.

In some of the most painful moments of my life I have also learned some of the most significant lessons of my life even though those lessons were couched in false accusation and surrounded by misperception and innuendo. Yet, in the end, I wouldn't trade those experiences for anything because God was at work even then molding me and shaping me for his glory, making me a more Christ-like reflection of who he is.

It all boils down to this. *Do you want to be right or do you want to be whole?* Do you want to be vindicated for all to see or is it okay if public vindication does not yet come your way but the pleasure of God is upon your life anyway? Which is more important?

John 18:11 contains the secret to overcoming the pain of betrayal and false accusation. Judas and his band of betrayers find Jesus in Gethsemane, Peter impulsively draws his sword, cuts off the ear of the servant of the high priest, and the Son of God responds to Peter: "Put up you sword into the sheath: the cup which my Father has given me, shall I not drink it?" *Shall I not drink it?!*

This rhetorical question is really a statement of fact. It is a statement in the affirmative by which Jesus gives full proof of his absolute submission to the Father's will. The Father had staked out the plan, predetermined in the annals of millennia past, and the Son would be faithful to the plan, becoming obedient "even unto the death of the cross." There could be no other course, no other action. *Peter, in the flesh, could not be allowed to come between the lips of the Master and the cup of the Father!* How often we become spiritually myopic, unable to see anything but our offender at the end of our own sword. How much bigger the Father's scope and vision!

What a remarkable pattern for us of unreserved submission to God's will in everything that concerns, even the very issues of life and death. The Father's will is much more than cash and cars, palaces and possessions, salaries and success, fame and fortune, tinsel and toys. What cup is the Father holding up to your lips this day?

L. E. Maxwell in his book *Born Crucified* explains: "Submission and suffering are utterly contrary to the flesh. The thing man loves more than anything else in the world is—himself."[4] If we are honest, we would admit that is also true of us. Jesus readily embraced all that the Father asked of him. He recognized that this particular cup came from the Father and he drank of it *willingly*—difficult though it was to swallow. "*Shall I not drink it?*"

Child of God—this speaks to us that we must live so near to heaven; that we must be so often in his holy presence; that we might easily discern the source of the cup and respond appropriately. The problem is, many times the Lord holds his blessed cup up to our lips and we rebuke it and turn away from it because we think it's of the devil!

We must learn to discern the voice of the Lord. He said himself, "My sheep hear my voice . . . and they follow me" (John 10:27). What does that say about the multitudes who claim to be his children but follow *other* voices into fields of false doctrine and pastures of materialistic greed and ego?

Let me ask you one immense and pivotal question. As you picture in your mind's eye Peter standing in the garden with blood on his dagger, a severed ear at his feet, anger in his heart, and the flesh in control—whom did he most resemble at that moment—Malchus, the servant, or Christ?

You see, it was *self* that propelled Peter into this predicament. How humiliated he must have felt as Jesus reached out and healed the ear of Malchus! Of all people! The one who had come to take the Son of God by force. But Jesus *healed him!*

Peter stands there with the flesh completely exposed. There had been no word from God to do such a thing, no command from Christ, no signal from the Master. It had been *Peter's* idea! It had been *his* fleshly impulse and he missed the Father's plan by a million miles!

Oh, but friend! Blessed is the one who can say in the heat of the trial as did our Lord, "The ruler of this world is coming. But he has no power over me" (John 14:30 CEV).

Examine our text once again and notice that Jesus fully discerned the source of his situation and responded with the

4. Maxwell, *Born Crucified*, 109.

THE SIMPLE POWER OF A BROKEN LIFE

appropriate grace. Verse 11 reads, "The cup which my *Father* has given me, shall I not drink it?" You see, there is really no other choice. Even in the valley of the pain of betrayal. Either I love him and obey, or I turn from him and disobey.

The great question of obedience for us today is simply this: "*Shall I not drink it?*" Are you fully surrendered? Are you totally obedient?

Madame Guyon, triumphant saint and mystic of the Middle Ages, claimed: "No man can be wholly the Lord's unless he is wholly consecrated to the Lord; and no man can know whether he is thus wholly consecrated except by *tribulation*. That is the test . . . he who does not welcome the cross does not welcome God."[5]

When we balk at the great testings of God we immediately injure our relationship. Remember, the Scripture reminds us in Hebrews (12:2) that "Jesus . . . for the joy that was set before him endured the cross, despising the shame, and is set down at the right hand of the throne of God."

Shall I not drink it? What is in *your* cup? What is the Master asking? You must cease from *your* way and *your* comfort, from *your* striving and *your* labors. Glorious, deliberate resignation—no higher form of faith than this!

My hope for you is that your season of false accusation will cause you to be *more* full of grace toward others and *less* critical of their shortcomings. You see, without grace we become judgmental and critical. Without grace we expect everyone else to be at the same level we are at. Without grace we have little appreciation for the growth levels of others. Without grace we place our own expectations on everyone else and then criticize them when they don't measure up.

Those who are type-A, task-oriented, driven people will tend to think in terms of black and white with very little grey area in between. Of course, I am not referring to morals or clear-cut biblical truth, but things in life and in Scripture about which there is no clearly defined answer. The older we get the larger our grey area needs to become and to a very great extent our success

5. Maxwell, *Born Crucified*, 106–7.

in life and our success as leaders is determined by our ability to navigate the grey areas. Friends—give grace! That must be at the very core of who we are as followers of Jesus. Grace! In the grey areas—let there be grace!

"The richest, the fullest, the most fruitful lives," intones M. R. DeHaan, "are those that have been in the crucible of testing, that have been broken upon the wheel of tribulation. We have no right to believe that God will do anything with our lives until He has broken us."[6]

This is what our Lord modeled for us in John chapter 13. Jesus, their master, their teacher, the Creator and life-giver of all things, the One who spoke the worlds into existence wrapped a towel around his waist, poured water into a basin, and began to wash the feet of the astounded disciples (vv. 4–5).

Then he unwrapped the lesson for them in the plainest of language: "If I then, your Lord and Teacher, have washed your feet, you also ought to wash one another's feet. For I have given you an example, that you should do as I have done to you" (vv. 14–15 NKJV).

My eldest daughter, Jessica, enjoyed a once-in-a-lifetime basketball season her senior year of high school. At six foot one, she was, in many ways, the heart and soul of that wonderful team that made it to the Final Four of the state tournament for the first time in school history.

During summer practices that year her coach (who is the winningest coach in Ohio high school history), endeavoring to motivate his captains, and by extension, the whole team, threatened one day that he was not going to have captains that year, because they were not putting forth sufficient effort. I asked Jessi what she thought of that when she came home and told us what had transpired. She blessed me with her response that showed depth of character and maturity of mind. With a shrug of her shoulders she simply stated: "That's okay. You don't have to have a title in order to be a leader."

6. DeHaan, *Broken Things*, 17.

Wow. You don't have to have a title in order to be a leader. Short and sweet. Deep and profound. Stunning in its simplicity, towering in its truth. Are you leading, friend? In spite of what others may or may not have said about you, regardless of things that may not have yet come your way—can you still lead and love? Can you wash feet? Can you serve behind the scenes? Can you perform the menial? Even without the accompanying title and tinsel?

Don't miss this: when Jesus washed their feet *Judas was still in the room!* Loving our betrayers is not easy. Overcoming the bite of their betrayal and the sting of false accusations is a challenge for even the godliest among us. And yet, we must. We *must!* For Jesus showed us *how* to do it and expects us *now* to do it. Such mind-blowing forgiveness only comes to us as we cry out to God for more of his grace, more of his mercy, more of *him* to flow through us that we might live as he commands us to live.

And the umbilical cord that keeps us connected to him, to his grace, to his power is prayer. Prayer is not given just for the crisis time, the emergency time, the "my life is out of control" time. Prayer is to be as natural a part of your day-to-day routine as eating and breathing. Abandon yourself to prayer. Learn the joy of that discipline. Be a person of prayer.

Yes, pray even for those who betray you and falsely accuse you. The whole teaching of Jesus on binding and loosing in Matthew 18 flows out of the context of forgiveness and reconciliation— i.e., communicating with God about people and situations that are false and unjust so that relationship might be restored. Let's take a fresh look at it in light of prayer.

In verse 15 we read: "Moreover if your brother sins against you, go and tell him his fault between you and him alone. If he hears you, you have gained your brother" (NKJV). Did you see that? "You have *gained* your brother." That is the main objective!

But in order to gain back our sister or brother we must care as much about the other person as we do our self. We must value relationship more than being right.

Then vv. 18–35 deal with forgiveness! The backdrop of this passage is church discipline (by the way, a church without discipline is not a New Testament church!).

Can you even begin to imagine what the kingdom could look like and what our communities could look like if, instead of using this passage to accumulate stuff and plead with God to grant our petty desires, we instead used it to develop the power of relationships!

Dare I say it? Binding and loosing is not about agreeing with a couple friends so you can have more things—it's about agreeing with friends for your relationships with others to be restored and healed! Get a couple of friends to agree with you that God will help you to forgive others. Gather prayer warriors around you that will believe God with you to change the heart of your unsaved spouse. Don't give up on that wayward child. Two or three brothers or sisters in Christ praying with you will bind the enemy's hand in that child's life and loose the power of God instead. *That* is the context and meaning of this passage!

ψ

A final word regarding David and the example he sets for us in seasons of betrayal. A very interesting story unfold in 1 Samuel 26 where David, wrongly hunted down—again, spares the wayward king—again. Remarkable in our own day, let alone in the kill or be killed world of David's day.

David and his nephew Abishai sneak down into the camp where Saul and his soldiers are camping for the night. Saul and his bodyguards are asleep in a trench with his spear stuck in the ground at the king's head. Abishai asks David to let him pull it out and thrust Saul through with it before he even knows what happens. David is both firm and clear in his refusal: "Do not destroy him; for who can stretch out his hand against the Lord's anointed, and be guiltless?" (v. 9 NKJV).

So David contents himself with instructing Abishai to take the spear and a jar of water and retreats back to the top of a nearby hill whereby he calls down to Saul and Abner, the king's top general. He challenges Abner as to why he has not done a better job of guarding the king. He humbly asks why the king is pursuing him.

Saul says that he has sinned and acted like a fool and erred exceedingly (v. 21). David responds with what is to me one of the most striking statements from his fascinating life. He simply says: "Your Majesty, here's your spear! Have one of your soldiers come and get it." (v. 22 CEV). Amazing! What do we glean from this brief exchange? What's the big deal about a new recruit climbing up to David to retrieve the spear?

First of all, the spear represented Saul's authority and belonged with its rightful owner. But second, and more importantly, *David did not want the slightest appearance of being a spear-thrower!* Do not miss this critical principle! Never give off even the *appearance* of being a spear-thrower! If David had simply thrown the spear three-quarters of the way back down to Saul, undoubtedly there would have been those who would have said: "I was there the day David threw a spear at the king and tried to kill him! I saw it with my very own eyes! " The false accusations would have flown further and faster than the spear itself!

How many times had David escaped that spear! And how many times had the Lord protected him from Saul's impudent rage! And now he would prove once and for all that he had absolutely no intention of harming his king. He would not give off the slightest impression of impropriety. No matter the spears that came his way, *he* would not hurl them back at his king—no matter the ingratitude and betrayal that accompanied their vicious, pointed tips.

Dear wounded reader, please never, ever become a thrower of spears. I plead with you to learn from the painful life of an unfairly accused shepherd living in wilderness caves to *not give the slightest appearance of being a spear-thrower!* Life is too short. The kingdom too valuable. Your destiny too important. I implore you—*don't pick up the spear!*

When you have been falsely accused focus on character— not the cause. Blame seeking keeps you rooted in the past and keeps your eyes off of the promise. Not only that, but a "get even" attitude will keep you from your destiny! You cannot fulfill your destiny while seeking to place blame! You can do one or the other, but not both.

The same with sympathy. The Lord is looking for surrender and many times we are looking for sympathy! Why? Because sympathy turns the attention on us and our natural inclination is to make it all about us! But a sweet spirit of surrender puts the focus on God. And by the way, that's where it belongs.

Chambers expounds: "God can never make us wine if we object to the fingers He uses to crush us with. . . . when He uses someone whom we dislike, or some set of circumstances to which we said we would never submit, and makes those the crushers, we object. We must never choose the scene of our own martyrdom. If we are ever going to be made into wine, we will have to be crushed; you cannot drink grapes. Grapes become wine only when they have been squeezed."[7]

Friend, God is using some wilderness cave experience to squeeze you. A cave in which the pain of betrayal and false accusation is all too familiar. But sweetness will one day flow from the press of your life. Trust him. Trust the heart of the Father for you—even when you may not be able to trust those around you. Your squeezing, your hour of crushing will yield tremendous things as the simple power of your poured out, broken life trickles through the winepress of his perfect will.

7. Chambers, *My Utmost for His Highest*, September 30.

7

The Pain of Personal Failure

—PETER

> The distinguishing characteristic of leaders is that they use their experiences as learning tools and they gain renewed motivation from their failures. Leaders are not people who escape failure, but people who overcome adversity. God doesn't squander people's time.
>
> He doesn't ignore their pain.
>
> —HENRY & RICHARD BLACKABY, *SPIRITUAL LEADERSHIP*

> As bullet from the barrel spent;
>> As sunlight through the curtain rent;
> So words, which once they've left the tongue,
>> Can never, ever be undone.

HOW QUICKLY STINGING WORDS can fly off of our tongue, piercing the spirit of another before they have even finished passing through the air! How deep the wounds they incur! Deeper still our regret for ever uttering them!

Somewhat isolated from other types of pain and standing off to the side by itself is the pain that *our own* poor choices have brought upon us and those we love. It's one thing to innocently be on the receiving end of pain inflicted by others or just life itself. It's quite another to wade into the dark tempest of pain because we have failed—morally, ethically, relationally, or spiritually. Dr. Sam

Chand submits that "failure is the womb of success" in his book by the same name. "I'm convinced that life isn't so much how we deal with success but how we respond to failure."[1]

Peter's story jumps to the forefront of the experience of personal failure. Peter, the friend who stumbled. Peter, the rock who crumbled. Truth is, we all identify with Peter. We all have *been* Peter.

Peter—the confident! Peter—the brave! Peter—the impulsive. Peter—the confused. Peter—the denier.

Luke records for us that after his third denial of Jesus "while he was still speaking, the rooster crowed. At that moment the Lord turned and looked at Peter" (22:60–61 NLT). He *looked* right at Peter! It was bad enough that he denied Jesus—and three times at that! But that look! *That* is what he could not get out of his head.

That look of sheer and total disappointment. That look that wanted so much more for Peter. That look that somehow still managed to convey such love, such understanding, such—what was it? Grace. *Grace!* That life-changing word that would rescue him from the depths of his own personal failure. No wonder years later that small but powerful word would show up ten times in his two short letters.

Chuck Swindoll speaks of "'grace killers' . . . who restrain and limit the dynamic potential of the Christian life . . . those who criticize, condemn, and crush our hopes of joyful living."[2] Maybe you know some of those folks. The weight of your own personal tragedy is heavy enough. But then the "grace killers" show up, ready to remove any last vestige of breath or hope or possibility that they find.

Never mind them. Pay them no attention. If you have failed in a personal way then it is not about them anyway. Your personal failure needs to be resolved first of all with the Lord and then second to those you have wronged. You owe no ransom to others who have only come to collect the bounty of your mistakes. Wasting time contending with such will only detract you

1. Chand, *Failure*, 7, 22.
2. Swindoll, *Grace Awakening*, ix.

from the more important business of getting right with God and the truly offended.

As someone who has a few years of experience under his belt may I offer you this advice? Rid yourself of negative, critical people! They will do nothing but help you to be a cheaper, shallower version of yourself.

"But we've been friends for such a long time."

I understand. I really do! But negativity is like carbon monoxide. It is a silent killer. It goes unnoticed and builds and builds and builds until suddenly, when you least expect it, it has taken the very life from you.

You will have quite enough to handle dealing with personal failure as it is, let alone if you are adversely affected by the negative and the cynical.

ψ

When David committed adultery with Bathsheba and then had her husband, Uriah, murdered he cried out in anguish his amazing song of penitence: "The sacrifices of God are a broken spirit: a broken and a contrite heart, O God, you will not despise (disdain, regard with contempt)" (Ps 51:17). This is one of the rare instances where the majority of Bible translations all say the exact same thing!

Sincerity, of course, is the first step on the path of restoration. "Contrite" may be defined as "penitent; showing sincere remorse." Once we have been faithful to honestly confess what we have done and expressed sorrow for our sin, we have the assurance that we are forgiven and the sin is washed away.

Beth Moore writes: "After the divine humbling and crumbling, the called [one] is sure he's blown it and it's over. He doesn't realize that only now is he ready to serve."[3] Learning and growing from personal failure can only be accomplished with a strong and firm faith. As you begin to deal with self, as you begin to deal

3. Moore (@BethMooreLPM), Twitter, October 22, 2013, 5:04 a.m., https://twitter.com/BethMooreLPM/status/392622589073309696.

THE PAIN OF PERSONAL FAILURE

with the flesh you will be tempted to walk away because the cost is simply too great. But here is the key—*the very pain we dread and at times resist is actually the means by which God brings his greatest blessings to our lives.*

A commitment to deal with self requires perseverance and a commitment not to quit. Not on your marriage, not on your ministry, not on your kids, not on the lost, not on your word, not on your commitment itself.

Inner transformation then becomes immensely more important than whether or not you are right. Being more like him is more important than being right. Being more like Jesus is all that matters! *After all, when it comes to dying to self we don't die to die, we die to live!*

I never knew either of my grandfathers. My mother's father died from a heart attack while at the throttle of the locomotive he was directing down the tracks when I was just a toddler. Fortunately, he turned away from the controls as he felt it coming on and the train was able to stop. My dad's dad died several years before I was born. Though he came to accept Christ as his Savior in his latter years, I am told that he had quite the temper on occasion. So did my father, who was a wonderful, godly man—but human, just like you and me.

Guess what I inherited? And guess what I have struggled with all of my life? Yep. Anger issues. Not often. In fact, rather infrequent. Most who know me would probably view me as pretty easy going, kind of laid back, friendly, etc. But losing my cool even once a year or every other year is still *way* too often. Yet, underneath the surface, down deep in the carnal aspects of the DNA passed on to my fallen human nature there exists an ability to blow up in ways that definitely are *not* honoring to Christ.

I had always felt immediate remorse whenever I had lost my temper (or found it, as some would say!) with someone. Mind you, we are not talking about anything criminal or violent in nature—just raising my voice and yelling—but that kind of behavior is not the self-control the Bible speaks of. I would always feel such shame and genuine repentance for my behavior coupled with a

THE SIMPLE POWER OF A BROKEN LIFE

very sincere commitment to not do it again. I will contain it, I thought. I will control it, I thought. I will manage it, I thought. The only problem was that by the time it started to happen again it was already too late to contain, control, or manage!

So, at forty-nine years of age (I never claimed to be the quickest learner!) I decided enough was enough. I enlisted the help of a wonderful counselor, brought my wife in on the process (and anyone else who wanted to help!) and, most importantly, took a long, deep, painful look inside. What I found was not pretty. Sin never is. In fact, it was quite ugly. Sin always is. My problem was not directed at others for simply making an honest mistake. Toward such I would be quite forgiving. Rather, I noticed that it happened when I felt I was being ignored, disrespected, blown off, etc. In short—marginalized and made to feel insignificant.

Where did *that* come from? I discovered that anger arising from feeling disrespected or ignored had its roots in insecurity. Yes, at forty-nine I finally admitted how insecure I was in some areas of my life. Even while pastoring a church of five hundred, serving on various local, state, and national boards and traveling the world preaching for Christ. But that wasn't all. I needed to go deeper still. If the anger came from insecurity, where did the insecurity come from? I didn't like what I found, for underneath the insecurity was pride—the original sin—and my only recourse for victory was to repent of pride (so subtle are its forms!) and *base my identity on who I am in Christ!* When you and I do that, it does not matter what others say to us or about us or what they may do to us. I am so grateful that although I am not perfect, his mercy and grace have set me free and lifted me to wonderful heights of joy that I had not known in this area before! I had to go inward before I could go upward. I had to cry out in sincerity before I could sing a song of victory. How marvelous is his grace in forgiving, empowering, and enabling us to walk in newness of life! Nothing less than the resurrection power of Jesus Christ! *We must die in order to live!*

Additionally, there must be a willingness to look deep within and really, truly deal with what you find there. You will not overcome what you will not confront! That's the reason many people will not go to counseling—they are afraid of what they will be confronted with. Rather than deal with it, they deny it and bury it.

And that is exactly why some of you have not yet received your miracle from the Lord—*you refuse to admit who you really are and what you really need!* You refuse to believe that you have a drinking problem or a drug problem—so there is no miracle of deliverance. You refuse to deal with your anger issues, preferring to blame it on someone else—so there is no miracle of peace. You refuse to admit a lifetime of bad choices—always deflecting personal responsibility—so there is no miracle of joy. You refuse to stop glancing at inappropriate things and you do not put proper safeguards in place to confront your lust—so there is no miracle of freedom. You refuse to view your attitude as the bitter, critical spirit that it has become—so there is no miracle of victory.

But dear friend, why not know your God in a deeper way and confront the issues you are ignoring? Even the gut-wrenching issues of your own personal failure. Stop dreading it. Stop denying it. Stop delaying it. Just *deal* with it!

You are going to have to confront it sooner or later anyway, you might as well take a step of faith, trust your God, and deal with the problem now! Know your God and face your giant now!

"Christian spirituality, without an integration of emotional health, can be deadly—to yourself, your relationship with God, and the people around you," enjoins Peter Scazzero. I identify too readily with him when he continues and confesses, "I know. Having lived half my adult life this way, I have more personal illustrations than I care to recount. . . . [But] true spirituality frees us to live joyfully in the present. It requires, however, going back in order to go forward . . . breaking free from the destructive sinful patterns of our pasts to live the life of love God intends."[4]

Listen. I get it. It's scary. Fears and doubts surround you when you even contemplate such an outlandish thing as looking inward and living a life of brokenness and transparency. But trust me—the most frightening step you will ever take is the first step toward admitting who you are and what you've done. So do it anyway.

4. Scazzero, *Emotionally Healthy Spirituality*, 7, 93.

ψ

When the suffocating sting of personal failure is about to over-whelm you, remember this powerful truth: *Leadership is born out of the fire*. Yes, even the fire of your own failure. *Especially* the fire of your own failure. Say it with me, out loud if possible: "I will learn from this. I will grow from this." Say it again so that your own ears can hear it: "I will learn from this. I will grow from this." The failure of your yesterday is the building block for your tomorrow! Don't waste your failures! Learn from them. Grow from them. Put them to use by investing in the life of another.

A missionary leader and dear friend affirms: "Don't let failure define you. . . . Neither the high nor the low moments occupy the majority of our lives and they do not define who we are. . . . When you define yourself by God's word, failures become detours, setbacks, and training grounds that help determine the person God wants you to be in His kingdom."[5] It is critical that failure never be permitted to take control of our thought-life. Occasional thoughts, mental glances, and reminders may briefly pass through, but they cannot be allowed to *control*. Not. For. One. Minute. As one leader of leaders advises: "Failure is an in-side job. So is success. If you want to achieve, you have to win the war in your thinking first. You can't let the failure outside you get inside you. You certainly can't control the length of your life—but you can control its width and depth."[6]

And as you pour yourself into those around you, something small, nearly imperceptible begins to happen. A tiny seed begins to take root beneath the smoldering ashes of your failure. It can't be seen at first, but with time and watered by the tears of your own remorse it finally pushes its way past the last layer of debris that keeps it bound.

Then, with the kiss of the sun upon it and the sweet dew of hope within it, it continues its journey upward, growing both in size and stature, and quality and quantity until at last it reaches

5. Smythia, *Barnabas Way*, 46–47.

6. Maxwell, *Failing Forward*, 68.

where it has never been before. Indeed, where *you* have never been before, influencing the world for the better. And exactly what is this thing of beauty born of anguish and pain? Nothing less than . . . *success!*

The story of your life, the wisdom gained from your tragedy, the compassion birthed from your brokenness now stands tall, erect, strong, and faith-filled as it reaches out to encourage others who must also walk this earthly path below.

Success is not measured by houses, cars, positions, IRAs, titles, trophies, or achievements. Success—*real success*—is measured by the journey. By lessons learned and love invested. Learning from mistakes and lovingly sharing those lessons with others are the foundations for a lasting legacy. Billionaires may die and pass on nothing. Paupers may die and pass on everything!

That "common" man who dies but leaves a legacy of love and character and integrity to his family? Success! That famous athlete, musician, or movie star who had it all and squandered it all? Empty! That one made drunk by the intoxicating stupor of worldly possessions who lived mostly to please themselves? Empty!

The simple power of a broken life is of infinitely more worth than the CEO, politician, doctor, or lawyer who stepped on others, injured and wounded people on the way to the top, then hoarded it all once they arrived there.

In one of my darkest and most painful days, my youngest son, Matthew, called to tell me of his and his sibling's support for me as I walked through the deepest ministerial crisis of my life. They offered love, affirmation, prayer, encouragement, and even finances, if necessary.

Then two days later he gave me something more wonderful than those priceless gems. He gave me truth. Deep-down, insightful truth. Straight from the reservoir of God's word, through the lips of a twenty-two-year-old. This was his text to me: "There is something spiritually large here. The enemy is very much present, I think. But we'll prevail. Our integrity sells for so little, but it is all we really have. It is the very last inch of us, but within that inch, we are free. You're still a very free man."

Right now in the darkness of your situation, right now in the murkiness of your pain and heartache, the Lord is at work preparing to reveal his light to you. You may not be able to see it. Most likely you cannot even feel it. But he *is* there, within your "very last inch," just the same.

Just as he was with Peter. Three days had passed—one for each of his denials—and an angel revealed himself to the three ladies that had come to the tomb of Jesus to anoint his body with spices. Out of all the wonderful things that emerged from that conversation one in particular stands out for our purposes here.

Mark 16:6–7 records for us that the angel said to them: "He is risen; he is not here. . . . Go your way, tell his disciples and Peter." And Peter. And . . . *Peter!*

Yes, Peter had failed. Yes, he had cursed and denied. Yes, he could be brash and impetuous. Yes, he had stumbled in the most personal and painful of ways. And yet the tender love of God reached out especially to Peter because the Lord knew both the depths of Peter's remorse and the heights of his future potential.

Wondrous, is it not, that just a few weeks later Peter would boldly and unashamedly stand in front of thousands of people, including many who were responsible for the death of Jesus, and unhesitatingly proclaim: "Repent, and be baptized, every one of you, in the name of Jesus Christ for the remission of sins, and you shall receive the gift of the Holy Spirit" (Acts 2:38).

Think of it! God took someone locked in a prison of painful, personal failure and chose him to preach the very first sermon of the New Testament church! From personal failure to powerful prophet! From defeat and despair to courage and conviction! From disappointment and grief to anointing and glory!

Oh, friend! Don't you see? That's not just Peter's story or a Bible story. Your heavenly Father longs to make that *your* story, too!

There is potential in your failure. You, too, may move from despair and disappointment to unspeakable joy and fruitfulness again. It is the enemy of your soul that haunts you with whispers that you will never be used again. That you have failed too many ways and too many times. That is neither the voice nor the plan of God for you.

There is a wonderful purpose waiting to emerge from the pain of your failure. So what is it? What has the Creator placed down inside of you? Do you know what it is? And more importantly, are you *fulfilling* that purpose?

Let's boil it down to its simplest form:

NO PURPOSE = NO SUCCESS

KNOW PURPOSE = KNOW SUCCESS

This is critical. A person without a purpose is not grounded, they are not anchored, they are not settled. They do not have a foundation to build any kind of success on.

Purpose is not merely decided upon. *Purpose is discovered.* Purpose is the incremental unfolding of God's will in your life.

Apple CEO Tim Cook recently delivered the commencement speech for MIT where he conveyed: "I was never going to find my purpose working some place without a clear sense of purpose of its own. Steve [Jobs] and Apple freed me to throw my whole self into my work. To embrace their mission and make it my own. *How can I serve humanity? This is life's biggest and most important question.*"[7]

To know God, to live for him, to serve others as a reflection of his love, to lay up treasure in his kingdom, to live for something bigger than yourself—*that* is living life on purpose. To truly be successful you must know your purpose and rise from the pain of your own personal failure.

Your success, God's plan for your life, the fulfillment of dreams long thought dormant are yet before you. Rise! To the task! Take one more step! Don't give up, don't give in. Not now, not ever! There is powerful potential in the sweet simplicity of your broken life.

7. Cook, "Apple CEO," emphasis mine.

8

The Pain of a Lingering Label

—John Mark

> The Christian faith makes it possible for us nobly to accept
> that which cannot be changed, and to meet disappointments
> and sorrow with an inner poise, and to absorb the most in-
> tense pain without abandoning our sense of hope.
>
> —Martin Luther King Jr., *Strength to Love*

"Quitter."

"Come now. You don't mean that."

"He is and I do."

"Paul, I understand how disappointed you were in him when
he left us before, but I truly believe Mark has grown since that
mistake. Let's give him another chance."

"I just can't, Barnabas. My trust has been broken and we don't
have the time or resources to invest in people who won't follow
through. The task is difficult enough as it is without workers jumping ship when the going gets tough."

"But you know his heart, you know of the call on his life. You
know he is capable and . . ."

"What I know," the fiery leader interrupted, "is that he quit
the last time and I'm just not convinced he wouldn't do it again,
given the right circumstances. I'm sorry, my brother, but I feel
strongly about this. My decision is made."

And so, two of the leading figures of the embryonic church agreed to disagree and parted ways. Paul chose Silas to go with him as he headed out for Syria while Barnabas took John Mark and sailed for Cyprus.

Which of them was right? Probably *both* of them, for the most part. Barnabas saw the person, Paul saw the mission *and* John Mark's premature departure a few years earlier.

Which left the young evangelist feeling marginalized, unwanted, and . . . *labeled*. Even his name—Markos, "a defense"—seemed to mock his attempt at redemption, for indeed, he had never felt so attacked, so minimized, so . . . well, *defensive* as he did right now. And it wouldn't go away. It just sat there. Ever present. Like a heavy, wet blanket that seemed to shroud his wounded soul. A loser with a lingering label.

The truth was, he *had* quit. He *had* abandoned the mission. He *had* left unexpectedly. But that was then. He had grown, he had learned, and he had stepped forward for service again.

But.

But he had a label.

A label from his past, or so it seemed, firmly affixed to his present.

Please understand this about labels—they *always* seem biggest to the one they are attached to! And heaviest. And never-ending.

Labels come in many forms. Addict. Alcoholic. Abused. Adulterer. Abandoned. Autistic. Abnormal. Aborter. That's just the "A's"!

You might be wearing a label right now. Divorced. Introvert. Backward. Overweight. Hyper. Cheater. Lazy. Liar. Coward. Unwanted. Gay. Felon. Failure. Sinner. Quitter. Mistake.

One thing about labels is that they almost always carry some degree of truth with them. Often, a *lot* of truth. Now some labels are nothing more than a mean-spirited, soul-crushing label that is simply and specifically meant to hurt and wound your person. But other labels have some basis of truth in their origin. John Mark had quit. True! And the label you wear (however secretly) emblazoned on your chest carries significant portions of truth as well.

You *did* do time for theft. True! Or, you *have* spent many years addicted to drugs or booze or gambling or porn. True! Perhaps your self-centeredness *did* lead to the demise of your marriage. True! You *have* failed at work or in business or in ministry. True! You *have* struggled with your weight or feelings of insignificance for most of your life. True! You *do* have an inferiority complex, you *do* wrestle with insecurity and anger. True!

And the brokenness that arises from your scarlet letter of shame has left you spiritually and emotionally emaciated and drained. You inwardly yearn to know, "Is there any hope for anyone with such a label as mine?"

Some of you don't even have the strength to do that. You are in absolute survival mode and emotional and spiritual health seems to have forever evaporated from the horizon of your now hopeless existence. You find yourself seemingly abandoned to the wounds and scars of your lingering label.

One of the church's great servants was Amy Carmichael, who was born in Ireland in 1867 and devoted over fifty-three years of her life (without a furlough!) to serving women and children in India. She spent most of her final two decades confined to bed as the result of a fall and ill health. Amma ("Mother" in Tamil) knew both the painful wounds inflicted by others as well as the scars of her own limitations. Because of her courage in rescuing children from slavery and forced prostitution she endured many threats against her person and her ministry. She humbly referred to the difficulties of missionary life as "a chance to die" and accorded that wounds and scars were simply a part of discipleship, a part of what it is to truly follow Jesus. Among the many gems she left behind in the legacy of her suffering and compassion is this, perhaps her best-known, poem:

> Hast thou no scar?
> No hidden scar on foot, or side, or hand?
> I hear thee sung as mighty in the land,
> I hear them hail thy bright, ascendant star,
> Hast thou no scar?

Hast thou no wound?

Yet I was wounded by the archers, spent,

Leaned Me against a tree to die; and rent

By ravening beasts that compassed Me, I swooned;

Hast thou no wound?

No wound? No scar?

Yet, as the Master shall the servant be,

And pierced are the feet that follow Me;

But thine are whole; can he have followed far

Who has nor wound nor scar?[1]

Friend, wounds and scars *will* be a part of your personal journey with Jesus Christ. Whether wrongly cast upon you by others,
thrust upon you by the circumstances of life, or as a result of your
own self-created label please process them, heal from them, learn
from them and grow beyond them.

ψ

Not only do labels seem heavy and based on some degree of truth,
but they l-i-n-g-e-r. They don't seem to go away.

Reality check. Ready? Those insecurities you wrestle with.
They didn't just pop up last week, did they? Chances are they
have come to visit you through the decades from time to time.
Lingering.

The abortion or divorce or abuse or affair or arrest didn't just
happen yesterday (for most of you), but happened ten or twenty
or forty years ago. Yet you still feel the shame and the pain of that
persistent stigma. Lingering. Whether the offender or the offended
it's there. Waiting. Whispering. Haunting.

Yes, you blew it with your kids a few years back or blew up at
a coworker last week. You have tried to apologize and make things
right, but there is an abiding whisper in your soul that you are

1. Carmichael, *Toward Jerusalem*, 85.

doomed for such behavior. An incessant voice that is always there to remind you just what a jerk you are. Lingering.

Poet Maya Angelou so beautifully points out that "history, despite its wrenching pain, cannot be unlived, but if faced with courage, need not be lived again."[2] Isn't it time you broke free from your label and started living the life God intends for you to live?

In order to break free from your lingering label you will need to commit to three crucial realities:

First of all you will need to come to terms with—you! Just be you. Just do you. Don't try to be someone else, don't try to walk in their shoes, do what they do, or wear their armor. Know *your* gifting and operate in the confidence of what God has called *you* to do.

You may not have someone else's talent—but use *your* talents. You may not have the head start in life that others have had—but use the start that was given to *you*. Your race may look different than another's—but run your race well. Stop trying to be your older brother or younger sister—just be you. Stop looking at others and feeling bad about what you do not have—be grateful for what you do have and use it for God's glory. Know the giftings that God has given to you.

Remember when David first stepped up to challenge Goliath? King Saul gave David his armor. But that proved much too unwieldy and cumbersome for the courageous youth. David took the armor off and used the tools and weapons he was most comfortable with—a sling and a stone—and the rest is history.

You see, Saul's armor only works for Saul—it doesn't work for you because it wasn't made for you. Not only will Saul's armor not work for you, it will actually make things *worse* for you! Just. Do. You.

Are you operating within the scope and parameters of what the Lord has called *you* to do? A call may be described as a clear, deep, intuitive sense that God has laid his hand on you for a specific and predetermined task. It is a "fire in the belly, a pull, a strange attraction."[3] The call is vital if you are to last. Experiencing

2. Angelou, *On the Pulse of Morning*, p. 13, stanza 26.

3. Kraft, *Leaders Who Last*, 78, 83.

a specific, personal call from God will enable you to persevere. *It is the call that will keep you when things get tough.* And it is the call of God on *your* life that will begin to peel the label of your past from the potential of your present.

Second, God will oftentimes call us to do things that others think cannot be done. Are you willing to risk looking foolish for Jesus' sake? A call is a haunting thing that is ever before you. It is *not* a destination you have arrived at. If you ever think you have "arrived" you are in big trouble!

The call of God leaves you unsatisfied with anything else in life. There is a divine compulsion that drives you into his will. Mark 1:12 records for us of Jesus, "And immediately the Spirit drove him into the wilderness." *The call of God takes away all other options!*

As he releases you from the chains of yesterday's labels he will also lead you into the reality of his will for you—*today!* Step away from yesterday into today! Move out of your history and into your destiny! Leave failure and receive favor!

Through faith even messes turn into miracles. One step at a time, one moment at a time. God gives us our destiny in glimpses— often through the valleys of our own failure and dysfunction!

But that label you once wore as a valid description of what you did or where you have been no longer needs to defeat you. Allow a *new* label to be created—one birthed out of the pain of your past and the hope of your future. Is there a dream, a destiny buried under the rubble of your failures? Allow the Holy Spirit to remove the former things and plant new seeds of life and possibility within.

Third, become an ardent learner. One of the best ways to learn is to fail. Failure can be the first step toward success. Learn from your mistakes. *Seek to be a great learner and a great thinker*—not just a great leader or a great manager.

Philip Yancey maintains, "The proof of spiritual maturity is not how 'pure' you are but awareness of your impurity. That very awareness opens the door to grace."[4]

---

4. Yancey, *What's So Amazing about Grace?*, 198.

Becoming a learner is vital to breaking off the labels of your past. Learn of yourself! Learn of grace! Without fresh insight, new perspectives, and increased wisdom your label is bound to remain.

The fact that you have just read this paragraph is probably a pretty good indicator that you want to grow beyond yesterday's lingering descriptions. Take heart! When we hear the name "Winston Churchill" we think larger-than-life, statesman, and hero of WWII. But *before* he wore that label there were scores of people who viewed him as a national liability and a failure. A biography of him written in 1925 accused: "It is doubtful if even Great Britain could survive another world war and another Churchill."[5]

Undoubtedly, you have your critics and detractors as well. They may have labeled you based upon some shortcoming in your past. Or perhaps they have misjudged and maligned you without any basis of fact for their malicious marker, their baleful brand.

Either way, please remember their arrows are not the determiners of who you really are. They do not have to determine your future. Those poisoned-tipped darts will not be the last word of your story and they cannot defeat you—even when they crush your spirit and pierce your heart.

ψ

I'll never forget the time I was preaching in the City Mission for the homeless in my hometown when all of a sudden the Holy Spirit poured this thought through me into the hearers: "Others may have put a label on you, but God does not. He does not see you that way. *God is not a label maker, our God is a label breaker!*" What a sense of hope and victory flowed into that room that night with that unwritten, spontaneous line in my message. God is not a label maker, *he is a label breaker!*

No matter what you have done, no matter where you are, no matter the brokenness you find yourself in today, he is *still* the God of second chances! God is a god of grace! His presence is a place where second chances come to life!

5. D'Este, *Warlord*, 299.

Don't stop trusting him now! Don't give up on your destiny! Don't allow the enemy to keep you from your greatest victory! In Luke 12:32 Jesus assures: "Fear not, little flock; for it is your Father's good pleasure to give you the kingdom." Don't miss this powerful truth from that one small verse: Jesus has no words of condemnation for them because of their size, rather, comforting words of assurance regarding their destiny! He is not looking to beat you up because of what you do not have or scold you and punish you because of things not in your possession. Rather, He longs to lovingly, tenderly point you toward a God-filled future—*your destiny!*

Is there a dream deep within you that needs to be rekindled? Is there a sin that needs repented of? Is there a relationship that needs reconciled? A marriage that needs healed? Is there a miracle in your house just waiting to be received? Our God is not a label maker, he is a label breaker!

ψ

That young man that Paul could not bring himself to allow to accompany him? The passage of time shows that he was able to move beyond his labels and become fruitful once again. In Philemon 24 he appears in Rome as a fellow worker of—Paul! The apostle also recommended him to the church at Colosse (4:10).

Further, Paul shows how completely that label had been removed from John Mark by asking Timothy to bring Mark to see him during his incarceration and final days in Rome. Where once he had been branded a quitter, now the aged apostle refers to him as "profitable," i.e., "useful."

Oh yes. One other thing. That well-known command of Jesus to "go into all the world and preach the gospel to every creature" (Mark 16:15)—that's his, too. That's right. The one rejected for being unreliable and undependable ended up breaking the labels of his past and wrote the second gospel that bears his name!

And may the Great Label-Breaker do all that and more for you! May he remove every brand and unholy imprint that keeps you in check and empower you afresh as you advance into a simple, powerful life of healing and purpose.

9

Your Rebirth of Power

We want to avoid suffering, death, sin, ashes.
But we live in a world crushed and broken and torn, a world
God Himself visited to redeem.
We receive his poured-out life, and being allowed the high
privilege of suffering with Him,
may then pour ourselves out for others.

—Elisabeth Elliot, *A Lamp unto My Feet*

In spite of the prevailing attitude of our culture, brokenness is God's pathway to blessing! There are no shortcuts, no alternative routes. Please do not despise your brokenness! It serves a greater purpose than you can ever imagine. David would one day rule Israel and three thousand years later is still revered as Israel's greatest leader. But David also lived in a cave of brokenness before he ruled the people.

The Apostle Paul wrote in 1 Corinthians 15:31, "I die daily." We die daily to be resurrected. What would our resurrected life look like if we died daily? And then what would our relationships look like? Tough questions, but is there really any difference in the way we treat one another and the way the unsaved treat each other?

I mean, seriously. Is the only difference between us and the world the fact that we don't cuss and swear in our dealings with people (usually!)? But if we ignore people rather than approach them in love; if we bury our feelings and our seething displeasure rather than talking things through; if we blow up in anger rather than exercising self-control; if we annihilate people with our tongues behind their back rather than speaking the truth in love are we really any different than the world?

I believe we can be different. In fact, I believe we *must* be different because we are *called* to be different! And that difference is found through daily abandon to the teachings of Jesus Christ. And this abandon is not a onetime event! A truly broken person will always come out of their breaking experience better than when they went into it. And that is how you can spot a broken person—their brokenness will be wrapped in grace. Grace that has been forged in the fire of adversity and purified in the furnace of affliction.

Repetition leads to success and genuine life change. Abandoning to a life of brokenness and transparency is all about radical change. Such abandon is all about inner transformation. Christ has not come to simply fix us up a little bit or help us with our Sunday clothes—*Jesus Christ has come into this world to radically transform our lives from the inside out!*

Therefore, I must ask—have you been so transformed? Have you confessed your sins and asked Jesus Christ to forgive you of those sins and invited him into your life as Lord and Savior? I did not ask if you go to church or believe in some "higher power." It is not about what denomination you belong to or where your parents took you when you were an infant. I am asking you if you have a personal—*a personal*—relationship with God. If in the honesty of your heart the answer is "No" or "I'm not sure" then pause right now, wherever you are, and invite Jesus into your life and ask him to forgive you of all of your sins. Do not wait until you are "good enough"—none of us are so that day will never come. Make him Lord of your life and allow his grace to begin to do what nothing else can do—transform you from the inside out.

In Romans 12:1–2 we find two of my favorite verses, as well as tremendous insight for authentic, lasting life change: "I beseech you therefore, brethren, by the mercies of God, that you present your bodies a living sacrifice, holy, acceptable to God, which is your reasonable service. And do not be conformed to this world, but be transformed by the renewing of your mind, that you may prove what is that good and acceptable and perfect will of God" (NKJV). Daily abandon is not a onetime event!

One well-known pastor and author challenges with these words:

> Many times behind the pretty smile, behind the Sunday praise, there is a person who's hurting. She's alone. His life is in turmoil. When someone is struggling, reach out. Be a healer. Be a restorer. Take time to wipe away the tears.
>
> Your job is not to judge. Your job is not to figure out if someone deserves something, or to decide who is right or who is wrong. Your job is to lift the fallen, to restore the broken, and to heal the hurting.[1]

Friend, reach out and bless another. Speak a word of hope to the downcast. A wounded warrior needs honor, not pity! Watch what honor does to a person who feels like a failure!

The healing of your marriage is not a onetime event. The process of relational reconciliation is not a onetime event. Becoming emotionally healthy is not a onetime event. In reality, after the reconciliation, that's where the hard work starts. Reconciliation means being more interested in restoration and relationship than it does being "pain free." Simply put, the things it takes to get healthy aren't necessarily fun. But they are well worth it. And they pay eternal dividends!

ψ

Something that we often wrestle with, which is juxtaposed to God's way, is the "comfortable way." This is the way we take just because it's what "feels" best for us. It's not a question of our body and the physical realm, neither is it a question of our mind and our thoughts. This is an issue of the will, an issue of *how we feel* and whether or not we will be ruled by faith or by feelings and the fear that feelings often bring.

1. Osteen, *I Declare*, 89.

One of the most common sayings by Christians in our day and age is "Well, I just have to do what is best for me." Most of the time that is code for "I want to do what *feels* right for me." We have bought in so much to the pop psychology of our day that we have forgotten to stop and ask ourselves one very important question: "What does the Bible say about this?"

The Bible never instructs us to live by our feelings. The Bible never tells us to live according to what we feel is best for us. The Bible never teaches us to put our will first. What if Christ allowed his feelings to take precedence over the Father's will? What if he had done what was best for him and avoided Calvary? Always, always, always the Scriptures teach us to ask this question: "What does God want me to do?" Jesus said in Luke 9:23, "If any man will come after me, let him *deny himself*, and take up his cross *daily*, and follow me" (emphasis mine).

The Apostle Paul was harangued by a tormenting spirit sent from Satan that constantly sought to distract and discourage him (2 Cor 12:7–10). Three different times he asked the Lord to remove this "thorn in the flesh." This spirit followed him, incessantly trying to disrupt Paul's plans, disturb his spirit, and defeat his divine mission. The Lord's answer to Paul's request is one of the most sublime passages in Scripture: "And he said unto me, My grace is sufficient for you; for my strength is made perfect in weakness." I love the way *The Passion Translation* expresses it: "My grace is always more than enough for you, and my power finds its full expression through your weakness."

There it is! "My power finds its *full expression* through your *weakness*." Your weakness, your lack, your inability, your limitation, your failure is *not* your ceiling—it is your opportunity for his grace, his wisdom, his power to be manifest in your life unlike anything you have ever seen before! That is why Paul went on to say, "Most gladly, therefore, will I rather glory in my infirmities, that the power of Christ may rest upon me. Therefore, I take pleasure in infirmities, in reproaches, in necessities, in persecutions, in distresses for Christ's sake; for when I am weak, then am I strong." Do you see it? Through the transforming power of the cross that reverses the laws of the natural, when we are *weak*, then a deeper unfolding of Jesus transpires in our life and we are *strong!* If—*if*—we will trust him through the painful process. It is then—in the valley of our deepest weakness, when our pain and brokenness is kissed by the majesty of his sovereignty and grace—that we find our rebirth of power.

Of course, this rebirth of power will also come along the lines of the "s" word—submission. The enemy wants you to doubt the power and mercy of God and will fight you vigorously along this line. But make no mistake, your ability to *possess* authority is in direct proportion to your willingness to *submit* to authority.

Christians around the world were shocked in early 2015 at the news that twenty-one brothers in Christ had been martyred in Libya because of their faith in Jesus Christ. The images of black-clad terrorists forcing their captors in orange jumpsuits to kneel in the sand with knives to their throats left indelible images in our minds. Especially when the video ended by showing the Mediterranean waves on the shore turning red with the blood of these brave and faithful men.

Twenty of the martyrs were believers from Egypt. One was noticeably different. An African, Mathew Ayairga, was not a Christian when he had been taken prisoner. But when the ISIS militants demanded that he, too, convert to Islam he refused. He had seen the courageous, unwavering faith of the Egyptians and decided to become a follower of Jesus as well. When asked shortly before his death "Do you reject Christ?" his response was bold and firm: "Their God is my God" and he received his martyr's crown along with the others.[2]

A few weeks later my wife was preaching and summarized their faith quite succinctly when she said: "The twenty-one totally relinquished control of the little things long before they ever knelt in the sand." How simple! How powerful! How broken! They totally relinquished control of the little things long before they ever knelt in the sand. And so must we. The battle isn't always with the big things, the large things. It is most often first fought in the small

2. Bos, "African Man Turns to Christ."

YOUR REBIRTH OF POWER

corners and insignificant recesses of our lives. We must be diligent and victorious *there* before we can conquer giants and subdue kingdoms. We must be consistent and faithful when no one is looking before we will be proven true in more public ways. Consistency in the small, the ordinary, even the mundane paves the way for deeper trust and yields sweeter fruit and blessing. Are you consistent in the little things? Have you relinquished all—*all*—for him? Your rebirth of power is just around the corner and will surely and absolutely come along the lines of submission.

Matthew 26:39 again sets the scene for us: "[Jesus] prayed, saying, O my Father, if it be possible, let this cup pass from me: *nevertheless, not as I will, but as you will.*" Friend, hear me—*the only true breeding ground for perfect peace is the will of God!* Isaiah 26:3 speaks to this: "You will keep him in perfect peace, whose mind is stayed on you, because he trusts in you."

So, here we are again. Back on familiar ground. Back on basic ground. I speak of the soil of obedience. The soil of submission.

Webster defines *submit* as "to present to others for consideration" and "to yield to the power or control of another." Through submitting, we release our authority and control and acknowledge a wiser, stronger, better authority than ourselves. But here's the key: *un*-submissive spirits can never be effective in the kingdom of God because *un*-submissive people cannot be trusted with the power of God!

Un-submissive people abuse power. They trample on others. They run roughshod over weaker ones and overpower those too naïve or timid to resist their allure. They seek to dominate and control. Control. *Always* they seek to control. They control with mind games. They control with passive-aggressive behavior. They manipulate feelings. They pretend to be sweet and innocent on the outside but are full of petty jealousy and insecurity on the inside. They firmly affix a super-spiritual facade to the stubbornness that quietly and continuously exists within. A thin veneer of reality hides the self-will, self-rule, and self-importance that dominate their thinking. They are empty. They are shallow. They are *un*-broken.

In startling contrast to these the pattern of Jesus Christ is *unrestricted submission!* The seventh and final cry from the cross was, "Father, I entrust my spirit into your hands!" (Luke 23:46 NLT). Submitting to Christ and allowing him to be Lord over everything—including our fears—releases us for greater usefulness. One well-known preacher of yesteryear alludes to this: "He was here before there was any fear and He will be here when all fear has passed away. Let us remember that He saw everything before there was anything. If we could stand at His side today and see what He sees, how baseless would be our fears and how excuseless our tears."[3]

Friend, when your world is caving in and the pain is more than you can bear, throw yourself into the hands of your loving heavenly Father! It is unsettling, I know. It is quite vulnerable, I know. I have been there! At the onset of what proved to be one of the most painful ordeals for me in four decades of ministry, terminated, feeling rejected, unwanted, and marginalized, and with a few false accusations thrown in for good measure, a dear friend blessed me with Pete Wilson's book *Plan B.* There I found these challenging words: "Joseph may have been stripped of his coat but not his identity. He may have been rejected and abandoned by his family, but he never stopped depending on his God. . . . He's making a choice to respond in all circumstances as if God is with him. . . . It's as much about the person we're becoming as it is about where we're going."[4]

Where are you going, my friend? Where will the current trajectory of your life lead you? Submission is both the most difficult and the most rewarding thing we do. Reading these words right now are people who have never completely submitted to the Lord (whether saved or not yet in a relationship with Jesus). Submission is a painful subject for you because you struggle with it, but it hasn't gone away *and it will not go away* until it is dealt with at an altar and crucified with Christ.

3. Havner, quoted in Ketcham, *Why Was Christ a Carpenter?*, 171.
4. Wilson, *Plan B*, 74, 79.

Recently Paulette and I hosted a married couple's small group in our home. One of the couples was going through a half dozen different and very serious trials, any one of which would have been painful enough on its own. Yet their faith was shining brightly as they shared of trusting Christ day by day by painful day. Then I heard these precious words flow from the depths and the lips of the wife: "Lord, I thank you for allowing all this stuff to drive me to my knees, to drive me to your feet."

To drive me to my knees, to drive me to your feet.

To drive me to my knees, to drive me to your feet!

Dear reader that *must* become our unfaltering pattern in life! A fiery furnace of affliction that drives us to our knees, that brings us to his feet. If you find yourself turning from that there is no other hope! Victory will not come from some other source, some other place. It comes from knowing *him!* Truly knowing Jesus and falling—yes, *falling!*—deeper into his arms of love.

In the mid-1990s, my wife and I and our four young children traveled from church to church in our home state of Ohio raising funds to live as missionaries in West Africa. Initially, we thought we would be living in Liberia,[5] a country that was somewhat emerging from, though still engaged in, a brutal civil war.

I had traveled to Liberia by myself two years prior and saw firsthand the devastation, destruction, and despair. No electricity. No running water. Every house along the beach for miles shot up and burned. Most government buildings pockmarked from automatic weapons and rocket propelled grenades, ransacked, and pillaged. No postal service. No banking infrastructure. The government barely functioning. The *country* barely functioning.

And here we were, thirty-five and thirty-one, respectively, with four kids ranging from one to ten. As you might imagine, my wife would sometimes be met with the question, "But what about your kids? What about their safety?" Paulette had wrestled

---

5. Because of unrest in the region, we ended up living in Senegal while I traveled into The Gambia, and the war-torn countries of Liberia and Sierra Leone. These were the days of dreadful conflict made famous by such films as *Cry Freetown* and *Blood Diamond.*

with this herself for the better part of three years before the Holy Spirit powerfully impressed upon her these peace-giving words: "The safest place for my children is for *me* to be in the center of God's will."

And so it will be for you as well. Your rebirth of power will follow the lines of your submission. The deeper you allow the Holy Spirit to take you in that area the deeper your reservoir of power.

Have you submitted to God's overarching plan for your life? Do you have at least a partial sense of what his vision is for you? Are you actively seeking to fulfill his will? Is there a great, single purpose to your life or is it hit and miss, scattered over many good things in many different directions?

ψ

The late Steve Jobs's name has become synonymous with creativity and cutting-edge innovation. While Apple's products spoke for themselves, Jobs's skills of persuasion may have always been what set him apart from other CEOs. When Jobs was recruiting Pepsi-Cola CEO John Sculley to come and work for Apple, Sculley was already leading a multimillion-dollar company and saw no benefit in leaving. But Sculley said that all changed after Jobs asked him one question: "Do you want to sell sugar water for the rest of your life or come with me and change the world?"[6]

Friend—do you want to drink sugar water for the rest of your life or do you want to abandon to Jesus Christ and help to change the world?! Do you want to continue to wallow in defeat, misery, and unending pain or will you allow the simple power of your broken life to magnificently impact the lives of those around you? *Never underestimate the power of a beginning!*

Andrew Murray was a South African author and pastor who exhorted: "Beware in your prayers, above everything else, of limiting God, not only by unbelief, but by fancying that you know what He can do. Expect unexpected things. . . . Think of what He

6. "John Scully on Steve Jobs," YouTube video, 0:46, posted July 31, 2010, https://www.youtube.com/watch?v=S_JYy_oXUe8.

can do, and how He *delights* to hear the prayers of His redeemed people. Think of your place and privilege in Christ, and expect great things! "[7]

We want deliverance from the trials and the pain. God wants the process. And in the process—even when you have no idea what to do next—worship. Just worship him. Faith must learn to tune the instrument of worship before receiving the victory.

In *The Fellowship of the Ring*, J. R. R. Tolkien offers these words of hope:

> All that is gold does not glitter,
> Not all those who wander are lost;
> The old that is strong does not wither,
> Deep roots are not reached by the frost.
>
> From the ashes a fire shall be woken,
> A light from the shadows shall spring;
> Renewed shall be blade that was broken,
> The crownless again shall be king.[8]

Dear reader, it is not always the stripped who are failures or the broken who are not whole. Man looks on the frail shell of the outward, but God ever, only on the heart. Your tears and your scars may very well be the only visible evidence of your private, personal victory, but knowing that he knows is enough. Therefore, stand! And fully embrace

The simple power of a broken life.

I bless you and I wish you well on your journey!

7. Murray, *Jesus Himself*, back cover.

8. Tolkien, "All That Is Gold Does Not Glitter," in *The Fellowship of the Ring*, 171.

Bibliography

Angelou, Maya. *On the Pulse of Morning*. New York: Random House, 1993.

Ash, Christopher. *Zeal without Burnout*. Surrey, UK: Good Book, 2016.

Augsburger, David W. *Caring Enough to Hear and Be Heard: How to Hear and How to Be Heard in Equal Communication*. Scottdale, PA: Herald, 1982.

Bevere, John. *The Bait of Satan*. Lake Mary, FL: Charisma House, 2004.

———. *Good or God?* Palmer Lake, CO: Messenger International, 2015.

Blackaby, Henry T., and Richard Blackaby. *Spiritual Leadership*. Nashville: Broadman and Holman, 2001.

Bonhoeffer, Dietrich. *The Cost of Discipleship*. New York: Touchstone, 1995.

Bos, Stefan J. "African Man Turns to Christ Moments before Beheading." Religious Freedom Coalition, April 24, 2015.

Carmichael, Amy. *Toward Jerusalem*. Fort Washington, PA: Christian Literature Crusade, 1988.

Chambers, Oswald. *My Utmost for His Highest*. New York: Dodd, Mead, 1935.

Chand, Samuel R. *Failure: The Womb of Success*. Niles, IL: Mall, 1999.

Chesterton, G. K. *What's Wrong with the World*. USA: Feather Trail, 2009.

Cook, Tim. "Apple CEO Warns about Tech's Downsides." *Fortune*, June 9, 2017. Summary of commencement speech at Massachusetts Institute of Technology, June 9, 2017. fortune.com/2017/06/09/tim-cook-mit-speech/.

D'Este, Carlo. *Warlord: A Life of Winston Churchill at War, 1874–1945*. New York: HarperCollins, 2008.

DeHaan, M. R. *Broken Things*. Grand Rapids: Zondervan, 1948.

Edwards, Gene. *A Tale of Three Kings*. Auburn, ME: Christian Books, 1980.

Elliot, Elisabeth. *A Chance to Die*. Old Tappan, NJ: Revell, 1987.

———. *A Lamp Unto My Feet*. Ann Arbor, MI: Vine, 1985.

Havner, Vance. *Hearts Afire*. Westwood, NJ: Fleming H. Revell, 1952.

Hession, Roy. *The Calvary Road*. Fort Washington, PA: Christian Literature Crusade, 1950.

Jackson, Dave, and Neta Jackson. *Heroes in Black History: True Stories from the Lives of Christian Heroes*. Bloomington, MN: Bethany House, 2008.

Keller, Timothy. *The Meaning of Marriage: Facing the Complexities of Commitment with the Wisdom of God*. With Kathy Keller. New York: Dutton, 2011.

Keller, W. Phillip. *David: The Time of Saul's Tyranny*. Waco, TX: Word, 1985.

Kendall, R. T. *God Meant It for Good*. Charlotte, NC: MorningStar, 1986.

———. *Total Forgiveness*. Lake Mary, FL: Charisma House, 2007.

Ketcham, Robert T. *Why Was Christ a Carpenter?* Vol. 2. Des Plaines, IL: Regular Baptist, 1966.

King, Martin Luther, Jr. *Strength to Love*. Minneapolis: Fortress, 2010.

———. "The Three Dimensions of a Complete Life." Sermon, delivered at Dexter Avenue Baptist Church, Montgomery, Alabama, January 24, 1954.

Kraft, Dave. *Leaders Who Last*. Wheaton, IL: Crossway, 2010.

Lewis, C. S. *The Problem of Pain*. San Francisco: HarperOne, 2009.

Lotz, Anne Graham. *Wounded by God's People: Discovering How God's Love Heals Our Hearts*. Grand Rapids: Zondervan, 2013.

MacDonald, George. *Unspoken Sermons*. New York: Cosimo, 2007.

Maxwell, John C. *Failing Forward: How to Make the Most of Your Mistakes*. Nashville: Nelson, 2000.

Maxwell, L. E. *Born Crucified*. Chicago: Moody, 1945.

McManus, Erwin Raphael. *The Last Arrow: Save Nothing for the Next Life*. Colorado Springs: Waterbrook, 2017.

Montgomery, Leslie. *Were It Not for Grace: Stories from Women after God's Own Heart*. Nashville: Broadman and Holman, 2005.

Mother Teresa. *Mother Teresa: Essential Writings*. Selected by Jean Maalouf. Maryknoll: Orbis, 2001.

———. "Mother Teresa's Humility List." Available online at https://www.catholiccompany.com/getfed/mother-teresas-humility-list-5880.

Murray, Andrew. *Jesus Himself*. Miami: Minerva, 2018.

Osteen, Joel. *I Declare: 31 Promises to Speak Over Your Life*. New York: FaithWords, 2012.

Rutland, Mark. *Dream*. Lake Mary, FL: Charisma House, 2003.

Scazzero, Peter. *The Emotionally Healthy Church: A Strategy for Discipleship That Actually Changes Lives*. Grand Rapids: Zondervan, 2003.

———. *Emotionally Healthy Spirituality: Unleash a Revolution in Your Life in Christ*. Nashville: Nelson, 2006.

Smythia, Isaac. *The Barnabas Way: A New Perspective on Biblical Leadership*. Published by the author, 2018.

Swindoll, Charles R. *The Grace Awakening*. Nashville: Nelson, 2010.

Thomas, Clarence. *My Grandfather's Son: A Memoir*. New York: HarperCollins, 2007.

Thomas à Kempis. *Of the Imitation of Christ*. Springdale, PA: Whitaker House, 1981.

Tolkien, J. R. R. *The Fellowship of the Ring*. Boston: Houghton Mifflin Harcourt, 1965.

Wilkerson, David. "The Making of a Man of God." Four-page printed newsletter of a sermon delivered May 27, 1991.

Wilson, Pete. *Plan B: What Do You Do When God Doesn't Show Up the Way You Thought He Would?* Nashville: Nelson, 2009.

Yancey, Philip. *What's So Amazing about Grace?* Grand Rapids: Zondervan, 1997.